THE DIVORCE LAWYERS' GUIDE TO
STAYING MARRIED

BY WENDY JAFFE, ESQ.

FOREWORD BY DANIEL J. JAFFE, ESQ.

VOLT PRESS
LOS ANGELES

THE DIVORCE
LAWYERS' GUIDE TO
STAYING MARRIED

10   09   08   07   06   1 2   3   4   5

Library of Congress Cataloging-in-Publication Data

Jaffe, Wendy.
  The divorce lawyers' guide to staying married / by Wendy Jaffe ; foreword by Daniel J. Jaffe.
      p. cm.
  ISBN 1-56625-268-7
  1. Divorce--United States--Anecdotes. 2. Marriage--United States--Anecdotes. I. Title.
  HQ834.J315 2005
  646.7'7--dc22

                                                              2005033857

Cover Design By: Candice Woo
Interior Design By: Joy Jacob

Volt Press
9255 Sunset Blvd., #711
Los Angeles, CA 90069
www.voltpress.com

For Jeff, Rachel, and Jake, with love

CONTENTS

ACKNOWLEDGEMENTS

To each and every attorney who shared their time and thoughts with me, please know that I am truly, truly grateful. This book only exists because of your enormous generosity.

I also extend my deepest gratitude to each of you who shared the intimate details of your marriages with me. Going through a divorce is difficult enough, re-telling your story so that others can learn from yours is downright brave.

Jeff Stern, my editor at Volt Press. You made a long-time dream come true. Thank you, thank you, thank you for trusting me with this book. And to all of the rest at Volt for transforming my words into a book including David Bell, Stephanie Penate, and Joy Jacob. Michele Weiner-Davis, your support has been a wonderful gift. Joelle Delbourgo thanks for trying, and for teaching me the book publishing ropes.

A huge thank you to my friends and family who make my life, my life. Carol Jaffe, they simply do not make mothers any better than you. Thank you for always being my cheerleader. And to my father, Dan Jaffe. I am both flattered and grateful that you trusted me with a lifetime worth of contacts. You represent everything that is right with the legal profession. To Barry Pressman, for always treating me like a daughter, and a special thanks to Steven Pressman for looking out for me like a sister when it came to finding a home for this book. Rob, Laurie, and Debs, siblings don't come any better than you guys. (And Debs, special thanks for the excellent pro bono editing). To all of my wonderful friends: I treasure each and every one of you more than you can possibly know.

Jeff, you have demonstrated again and again that when you said for "better or worse" you actually meant both. Thank you for your unwavering support of all my projects. Rachel and Jake, I am the luckiest person in the world because I get to be your mother.

FOREWORD

BY DANIEL J. JAFFE, ESQ.

In my forty-plus years of practicing divorce law, I have witnessed numerous marriages that could have been saved. I'm not talking about the clients who wish to end a marriage marred by physical abuse, and/or chronic alcohol and drug use that hasn't responded to treatment. I'm talking about all the rest. It is the clients who complain that they were unable to communicate, had a terrible sex life, were always fighting about money, had issues with a stepchild, hate their in-laws, live with a workaholic, are golf widows, are married to a wife who doesn't do anything but lunch and shop, live with a spouse who hollers at the kids all the time, or had an affair with his secretary/her trainer, that could have and should have solved their marital problems before they reached the point of divorce.

Wendy Jaffe's research has led her to the inescapable conclusion that it is the divorce lawyer, who during the course of divorce proceedings, lives with their client and learns the most intimate details of the client's marriage, and witnesses how a couple interacts during settlement negotiations and other divorce related activities, who can give valuable insight to spouses on how to make their marriages work.

Numerous books on how to create a successful marriage have been written by therapists who can only base their conclusions on their individual experiences with a limited number of couples in marital therapy. This wonderful book bases its conclusions on advice gathered from one hundred of the top divorce lawyers in the country whose combined thousands of years of experience dealing with parties at the end of their marriages gives a new perspective on marriage never before attempted.

My typical Beverly Hills divorce practice has dealt primarily with the rich and famous. These privileged people have had the benefit of being able to seek the guidance and help from the best marriage counselors available. Yet, when they finally come to my office to end their marriage and divide up their wealth and, unfortunately, their children, it was obviously both too little and too late. It is the rare situation when someone who decides to terminate their marriage and visits an attorney to facilitate that goal ever changes their minds and returns to the marriage.

I have often thought that the first item of personal property that a couple should discuss dividing is their wedding pictures. They should look at the pictures and ask, "Is this person that I married the same person that I am now divorcing?" In many cases the answer will be no. The young lady in the picture was not a mother, or a professional woman, or a consummate shopper. The young man in the picture was not a father, or a CEO of a large public company earning a multi-million dollar salary.

What could these same people have done during their marriage that would have accommodated these major life changes and permitted them to accept and adapt to the changes that time inevitably brings to all human beings? The clear answer is that they could and should have anticipated these potential changes at the outset of the marriage. This book teaches couples how to anticipate these changes and other marriage busters so that they can be addressed before they lead to divorce.

I draft many premarital agreements for couples that plan on remarrying after a divorce. Frequently, my clients ask me to add a clause (which legally would not be enforceable) about an area of behavior that plagued an earlier marriage. "Dan, put in something about if he/she starts drinking or doing drugs again then I will get the house, the boat, or the kids." Or, "I want him/her to agree that I will have equal access to all of our finances, that we will divide all of the childcare and housework, or that we will have sex at least twice a week, etc."

Of course, promises such as these made in a premarital agreement will not compel a party to live up to these agreements any more than the promise to love, honor and obey given in the marriage ceremony will be honored. A divorce lawyer's job cannot be the enforcer of promises people make to each other before entering into the bonds of matrimony, but divorce lawyers are an invaluable resource of knowledge of why marriages fail, and what a couple can do to make their marriage successful.

Read this excellent work and take advantage of the knowledge gleaned from one hundred professionals who have learned the intimate details of hundreds of thousands of marriages that have failed. Recognize the warning signals early and deal with those issues before becoming one of our clients, and a divorce statistic.

INTRODUCTION

"Divorce law is a very, very, very human field. Not a week goes by without someone screaming, crying or breaking down. Divorce lawyers deal with people at their worst."
Marshal Willick, Las Vegas, NV

❖

When you are the daughter of a Beverly Hills divorce lawyer, you grow up listening to stories of failed marriages. There was the one about the woman who assumed that her relationship was solid until she listened to the messages on her answering machine and heard, "Debbie, I will not be home for dinner....OR EVER. Click." I was captivated by the tale of Mr. and Mrs. Doe who spent thousands of dollars in legal fees fighting over a sentimental object that would bring $5.00 at a garage sale. My favorites were always the classics: the doctors who fell in love with their nurses, and the rich country club women who ran off with their tennis pros.

It wasn't until I followed in my father's very large footsteps and became a lawyer myself that I truly understood that behind every divorce petition was a real couple that had exchanged rings and promised to love and cherish each other forever. Wives and husbands checked the box on the divorce form marked "irreconcilable differences," but that didn't begin to explain how their hopeful "I do" was transformed into a bitter "I don't." I wanted to know how a couple went from calling each other "baby" and "sweetheart" one day to "plaintiff" and "defendant" a few months, years or decades later. Or, as one of the attorneys who participated in the making of this book colorfully put it: "These people have seen each other naked, a lot of times, and now they are in the courtroom calling each other Mr. and Mrs. Smith."

To find out why nearly half of all marriages fall apart long before death do us part, I interviewed 100 of the top family law experts in the country. Next, I interviewed dozens of people who had never expected to get divorced, but did.

Each attorney interview began with a deceptively simple question: "What are the reasons that people get divorced?" Their reasons were a lot more varied and complicated then we have all been led to believe.

Take two commonly assumed marriage breakers: infidelity and money. Just stop the cheating, get a raise, and presto, you have the recipe for the "perfect" marriage, right? Wrong. The lawyers that I spoke to explained *how* money and sex, and seven other factors act to cause the destruction of marriages. They also taught me something else, and that something else is why you need to take the advice of these lawyers to heart.

Nearly every lawyer I spoke to said that many of the people who came to them for a divorce could have saved their marriages if they had actively worked on the problems that plagued their marriages before they had gotten out of hand. JoAnn Reynolds, a Portland attorney who has practiced family law for more than twenty years said: "People don't go to marriage counselors until they are well on their way to seeing a divorce lawyer, and by that time it is too late because the unhappy spouse has already emotionally left the marriage."

And nearly every one of the divorced people who shared the stories of their failed marriages told me that they saw many of the problems that ultimately destroyed their marriage early on, but let those problems slide to the point where the marriage was irretrievably broken. "We went to therapy, but I was already mentally checked out of our marriage because the problems had gone on for so long. I think if we had received help when the problem first surfaced, we would still be married," one said. Another said, "I was working my butt off in therapy but my wife, who had begged me for years to go to counseling, didn't want to do the work. She said it was too late for her."

Learning to Identify and Treat the Symptoms of Divorce

We all know that early medical treatment is critical to preventing larger health problems down the road. Little Suzy is not an eloquent speaker by age three? She is off to a speech therapist because her parents know that early intervention can make a difference in her long-term prognosis. Feel a tiny lump in your breast? A mammogram is scheduled that day. Chest pain? Straight to the emergency room. Never have I heard someone say that they will have their doctor check out a growing mole after the kids are off to college, but people adopt this "wait and see" attitude with their marital problems. Venting your marital complaints to a friend over a latte at Starbucks may be momentarily therapeutic, but it doesn't get to the root of the problem.

Divorce has symptoms which, if left unchecked, will ruin your marriage. The key is to learn how to identify and then treat the symptoms. Doing nothing is only an option if you do not care whether or not your marriage works. This book will teach you how to recognize the symptoms that lead to divorce, and will identify the steps necessary to affect a cure.

How To Use This Book

The book works like this. Each chapter identifies a cause of divorce, relevant symptoms, and a series of questions directed to you, the reader. If you are experiencing specific problems in your relationship—whether you are already married or are in a relationship that you feel might lead to marriage—feel free to locate the chapter relevant to that problem and begin there. For example, if you suspect that your spouse or significant other is an alcoholic, or abuses prescription (or non-prescription) drugs, begin with Chapter 6. If you are experiencing problems in the way that you and your partner handle money, feel free to turn directly to Chapter 3.

If after reviewing the symptoms for a cause of divorce, and answering the questions in that chapter, you feel that the symptom is applicable to your relationship, you must "treat" the symptoms of that cause of divorce until they are gone. Treatment may include self-help and/or outside help. Suggestions on where to find the help that you need are included toward the end of each section.

Of course, you are welcome to simply start from the beginning of the book and read to the end. Ultimately, it will benefit your marriage to read about every symptom of divorce whether or not you feel that it is relevant to your relationship today.

The Divorce Lawyers Who Made This Book Possible

The divorce lawyers interviewed for this book are some of the very best in the country. They all practice family law exclusively. Most are members of the very selective American Academy of Matrimonial Lawyers and/or have been certified by their state bar organization as a family law specialist. Their names appear repeatedly on the "best lawyers" lists. While many of their clients are *People Magazine* regulars, CEOs of huge companies, and famous athletes, they also represent people just like you.

Cumulatively, the attorneys that participated in the making of this book have more than 2,500 years of combined family law experience and have participated in the divorce of literally thousands of people. They generously donated tens of thousands of dollars of attorney time to the making of this book with the hope that you will take their insights about divorce and use them to fix the problems in your marriage.

Although there are many terrific divorce attorneys who hail from my home state of California, I felt that it was important to interview divorce lawyers who practiced in every major region of the country. While every single attorney interviewed—whether their practice is based in Cleveland, Manhattan or Atlanta—mentioned some universal causes of divorce, certain marriage-busters were mentioned more often in specific geographic regions. For example, an attorney that practices in Miami spoke of the negative influence that Hurricane Andrew had on many marriages. Lawyers in the Northwest described how dot-com mania and the subsequent burst of the tech-bubble impacted marriages. Lawyers in New York and Washington, D.C. told of the impact of the terrorist attacks on already shaky marriages. I learned about marital issues that arise frequently among Mormons from an attorney practicing in Utah. An attorney practicing in Alabama talked to me about family law issues that were unique to the Bible Belt.

The lawyers interviewed for this book frequently commented that while they saw many marriages that were irretrievably damaged, they handled several divorces a year where the couple ultimately realized after the divorce that they should have worked through their problems and stayed married. Unfortunately, the divorce experience itself frequently caused those same couples so much pain that a healthy marriage could not be resurrected. Stated another way by attorney Mike McCurley from Dallas, Texas, "If we put half as much effort into being married as we do into getting divorced, the divorce rate would be cut in half."

Emily Behr, an attorney practicing in Atlanta, summed up the task of those wanting to stay married for life this way. "All marriages have cracks, there is no such thing as a perfect marriage." The real issue, she said, is "whether or not the couple handles the problems that occur."

Near the end of many of my interviews, the attorney and I would chat about marriage in general. Contrary to what you would expect, the divorce lawyers that I consulted with had a very positive view of marriage. Many were in long marriages themselves, and I heard over and over again how working with people going through divorce only made them work harder on their own marriages. Santa Monica attorney Scott Weston told me that as a married divorce lawyer, he observes his clients' mistakes and makes a mental laundry list of things that "he doesn't want to do wrong" in his own marriage. "I want to be a role model for my kids. I am a better parent for seeing the custody fights and a better husband for seeing the bad cases." I was repeatedly told by other family law attorneys that divorce work made them realize that "the grass is not greener on the other side of the fence" so they figured they might as well pull their own marital weeds and stick with the grass that they already had.

The lawyers I spoke to often had different points of view on the causes of divorce, but on this they were unanimous: learn to identify the symptoms of divorce and seek treatment immediately. Treatment may range from simply recognizing the problem and working with your spouse to change the behavior, to finding a therapist who helps solve (as opposed to merely discusses) marital problems. Remember early detection of symptoms is the key to making it to your golden anniversary just like early detection of disease is the key to making it to your golden years.

ONE
DIVORCE SYMPTOM #1: **SEX**

"It is rare that someone who is having good and regular sex will come to me for a divorce."
Maurice Kutner, Miami, FL

"When it comes to sex, people think that whatever they do is 'normal.' People will say, 'just the usual, once a month' or 'just the usual, twice a day.'"
Errol Zavett, Chicago, IL

❖

The irony about sex is that it is frequently the catalyst for both marriage and divorce. Intense sexual chemistry has sent many an otherwise incompatible couple down the aisle. According to my mother and her friends, many people got married in the 1950's because marriage was a prerequisite to sex. Even after the birth control pill prompted the sexual revolution of the 1960's making pre-marital sex the rule rather than the exception, people still seem to confuse sexual chemistry with love and compatibility.

I was not surprised to learn from the divorce lawyers that I interviewed that sex (or a lack of it) plays a role in divorce. I imagined that I would hear over and over again about the husband who had an affair with a younger woman, the distraught wife who found out, and the divorce that followed. But that is not what I was told. It seems that the role between sex and divorce is a lot more complicated than most people think.

Nearly every divorce attorney that I spoke with felt that infidelity, in and of itself, did not cause divorce. Marriages that were susceptible to infidelity—not the one night stand or sex addict variety, but the "I fell in love with someone else" model—usually already had other significant problems. In fact, many times the lawyers noted that the "victim" spouse wanted to stay married even after he or she knew about the infidelity, but that the cheating spouse wanted out.

Another surprise was that nearly every attorney that I spoke to emphasized that the impression that infidelity is a "male issue" is no longer correct. As women have become more prevalent in the work place, their rates of infidelity have increased substantially. While polls frequently rank men's rates of infidelity higher than that of women, the divorce lawyers that I interviewed believe that the infidelity gap between the sexes has narrowed to the point that it no longer exists.

I learned something else about the connection between sex and divorce that I never suspected. Many divorce clients confess to living in a sexless or nearly sexless marriage for years. You read that right. Not days or weeks without sex, but many, many years. Errol Zavett, an attorney practicing in Chicago, told me about a case he handled where the couple had been married twenty years and had never consummated their marriage.

Then there is the not so surprising effect that the internet is having on an already high divorce rate. It has made infidelity both more convenient and more discoverable, and pornography obsessions more prevalent.

Finally, I learned that a small, but not insignificant number of divorces are caused by sexual secrets ranging from cross-dressing to a change of (or admission to) a different sexual preference. (For issues related to marriages where one spouse is gay, please refer to Chapter 8, Growing Apart).

Cynthia Greene, a divorce attorney based in Miami, told me that if she were writing a book on the causes of divorce, she would warn married couples about the relationship between sexless marriages and divorce in "Chapter One." I am taking that smart lady's advice.

Low and No Sex Marriages

"I hear a lot—and I mean a lot—of people saying that they haven't had sex in years and years, and then being surprised that their marriage is ending. Twenty-five to fifty times a year, clients tell me they haven't had sex in two years, five years, or seven years. We are not talking about 'he wants it all the time.' We are talking about none… zero. If you are married to a healthy person and you haven't had sex in five years, and your spouse isn't protesting, there is someone else!! Hello!!"
Cynthia Greene, Miami, FL

"I handled a case where the couple hadn't had sex in at least fifteen years. For healthy people to go five, ten or fifteen years without sex was initially a shocker to me but it isn't anymore." Bill Hunnicut, Denver, CO

"I see a lot of libido problems. And lately it has been the woman complaining that her husband has lost interest." Donn Fullenweider, Houston, TX

Suzanne and Eric

Everyone thought that Suzanne had a "perfect" marriage. From the outside, it appeared that Suzanne, a petite brunette, and her athletic husband, Eric, were very connected. On the weekends they could be found on the tennis courts or cheering on one of their three children at the baseball field. They "did everything together" and never exchanged a cross word in public. Imagine the chaos that ensued when Suzanne left her husband "out of the blue."

When I interviewed Suzanne I quickly learned both why her marriage failed and why her community of friends and family were caught off guard. She had not shared her true feelings about her husband with even her closest friends. The truth, which Suzanne had kept hidden for years, was that she was not attracted to her husband and did everything to avoid being touched by him. And it was this way from the beginning.

Suzanne and Eric first met in 1985 when Suzanne was 21 and Eric was 23. Eric was studying to be a doctor, and Suzanne was training for a position in the medical field.

She explained, "I knew from the very beginning that something was missing; that something important just wasn't there. But at the time I was concerned about a bigger picture that included stability, a good family life, travel, and financial security for the future. We both tried to model our relationship after his parents' marriage, which, at least from the outside, appeared to be very strong. I had come from an unstable home and his parents' life and lifestyle really appealed to me."

"Our sex life was an issue from day one. Sex was a huge source of tension in the marriage. My husband just assumed that I was asexual, which wasn't the case. I just wasn't attracted to *him*. My feelings toward him were more how one would feel toward a good friend. It was work on my part to have any sort of a sexual relationship with him. I would always look for excuses not to have sex once we were in bed."

Suzanne and Eric's low sex marriage lasted fifteen years before Suzanne finally had enough. "We went to visit my parents who have a very antagonistic, disrespectful relationship. I think that was the straw for me. I didn't want to continue in a marriage to someone I wasn't in love with and wasn't attracted to. I didn't want to end up like my parents."

Steve and Linda

Many divorce lawyers said that they saw many women like Linda in their office; women who had a very low-sex marriage but didn't think that it was a "big problem." When these women learned that their husbands were being sexually fulfilled, but just not at home, they were frequently shocked.

Here is what Steve told me about his marriage to Linda.

"When Linda and I met she was 25 and I was 26. We both were on the executive track, and had the same interests. We both loved the Chicago White Sox, and had similar upbringings. In a million years, I never thought that we would get divorced.

"We had three kids in six years, and moved from the city to the suburbs. We did all of the typical stuff: little league, hung out with friends, and went to the movies. In fact, from the outside, things could not have looked more normal. What I didn't think was normal was that our sex life had slowly dwindled to practically nothing.

"Linda had gone back to work when the kids were in school fulltime. She had a pretty hectic day. She would leave work at five, stop at the market, and make all of us dinner, and then there was homework, piano lessons, etc. We would pretty much end up in bed together at around ten.

"After our first child was born, Linda went from someone who had been pretty interested in sex, to someone who could care less about it. We were not one of those couples who didn't have babysitting and could never go out without bringing a baby. We had a regular babysitter who came every Saturday night and we would go out with each other or friends.

"Even when we would have a great kid-free time on Saturday nights, she still would not be interested in sex when we got home. I asked her repeatedly if there was anything wrong, or if I had done anything, but she swore that there wasn't. She would just say that she didn't feel very sexual, but that she didn't know why.

"Our sex life went from about twice a week at the beginning of our marriage to about once a month if I was lucky. The problem wasn't just the frequency. It was completely obvious that if I never made a move we would *never* have sex. I didn't really get it because in nearly every other way we were really on the same page.

"I asked her to talk to her gynecologist about her low sex drive but she never did. I honestly think that it just wasn't important to her and she didn't realize how important that it was to me. By that time we had been married for fifteen years. Some of my guy friends were complaining about the same thing so I thought that maybe it was just "normal" after a certain number of years of marriage. But I did know some guys who said that they were still having sex with their wives a couple of times a week.

"I remember thinking that I didn't want to go the rest of my life without a sex life. I was in my mid forties, married to an attractive woman, had three great kids and the house and all of the other stuff that you are supposed to want. Yet I was really unhappy. Linda and I started fighting about stupid things. I admit that I started most of the fights but I really resented Linda for ending what was really an important part of our relationship.

"As the kids got older and started getting their own lives, I started spending more time at work. I pretty much figured that I would stick it out until the kids were in college and then I would leave. Most of the guys that I knew who also had bad sex lives pretty much "solved" their situations by having affairs. I didn't want to do that because I thought if the kids found out they might disown me.

"When my youngest was wrapping up his senior year in high school, I met someone at work who was very attractive and really came on to me. We started going out for dinner but I told her that there was no way I was cheating on my wife. She said she respected that and we went out for a few more months and really just talked. In a way, that turned out to be worse than having an affair because I ended up really falling for her. Finally, one day she just came in my office and closed my door and started kissing me. That went on for about five minutes. I realized that I had really strong feelings for this woman and that if there would be any possibility of a future with her, I would have to do things the right way. I told her that I was going to tell my wife that night that I was leaving, and that is what happened.

"Linda was absolutely shocked. I think now she realizes how much we had drifted apart, but at the time she was completely amazed that I would want to leave. I think because the facade was good, she assumed that everything was fine. She suggested that we try therapy first, but I felt like she had her chance to fix things years ago when I had suggested that she talk to her gynecologist. Plus, I had been checked out of the marriage mentally for so many years, I didn't think that therapy would do anything."

When I asked Steve if, looking back, he would have done anything differently, he said, "Yes. There is a lot I would have done differently. I should have insisted right when we started having sex problems that we see a therapist. I don't know exactly how, but I should have made Linda realize what a big deal our sex life was to me because her lack of interest really caused so much resentment on my part."

Lack of Sex is a Major Symptom of Divorce

"Sex is a big problem with a lot of my clients. A lot of them say sex is nonexistent. I am not sure what the cause and effect is there: Is the sex nonexistent because their marriage has gone down the tubes, or has their marriage failed because there is no sex? I think lack of sex is just another symptom that appears when the marriage has gone bad." Wolfgang Anderson, Seattle, WA

A low (or no) sex marriage matters if having a sex life is important to one of the spouses. This is not just a male problem. Many attorneys told me that an increasing number of their female clients are complaining about low or no libido husbands.

Nearly every attorney that I spoke to told me that they almost never see marriages split up where the couple's sex life is good. (Although David Walther, an attorney practicing in Santa Fe, New Mexico told me that he had one client whose wife was having an affair, who said that he hoped that "I can still sleep with her after the divorce.")

Of course, there are a lot of chicken and egg issues with sex: did the poor sex life cause other problems in the marriage or did the other problems in the marriage cause the couple to stop having sex? Ultimately, neither the chicken nor the egg is important. What is important is that every couple needs to realize that when both people in the marriage are healthy (and if lack of sex is an issue in your marriage, you should rule out any physical factors with your doctor), that lack of sex frequently leads straight to a divorce lawyer's office.

Symptoms

- Do you and your spouse rarely (or never) have sex?
- Do you or your spouse think that it is "normal" to have a healthy marriage that doesn't include sex?
- Do you or your spouse frequently complain about the lack of sex in your marriage?
- Do you not have sex with your spouse because you are no longer attracted to him or her?
- Is sex missing from your marriage and does your spouse frequently view pornography without you?
- Is sex missing from your marriage and do you have reason to suspect that your spouse is having an affair?

Cure It

There are just two steps that are involved in solving the low or no sex marriage.

1) Recognize that sex is a big deal.

Many people are surprised when their spouse cites a poor sex life as the reason that they no longer want to be married. Even if sex is not important to you, you have to realize that it might be extremely important to your spouse, and that it is a significant cause of divorce.

2) Get help.

Find help either through a book, a therapist, or both. Some books that you might find helpful are:

The Sex-Starved Marriage: Boosting Your Marriage Libido
By Michele Weiner Davis, Simon & Schuster, 2004

Rekindling Desire: A Step-by-Step Program To Help Low-Sex and No-Sex Marriages
By Barry and Emily McCarthy, Brunner-Routledge, 2003

I'm Not in the Mood
By Judith Reichman, M.D., HarperCollins, 1999

Infidelity and Divorce

"Infidelity is symptomatic and not causative. I have never met anyone who admitted to me that they woke up in the morning and thought, "You know, I think today I will have an affair." Stephen Arnold, Birmingham, AL

"The biggest problem with affairs is the couple doesn't take the time to get to the root of why the affair took place." Lowell Sucherman, San Francisco, CA

"Kids don't necessarily care if there has been an affair. Typically, they just want their parents together." Joanne Ross Wilder, Pittsburgh, PA

Nearly one hundred divorce attorneys agreed on this. While many of their clients blamed their divorce on infidelity, the infidelity itself wasn't the "cause" of the divorce. Stated another way, divorce lawyers rarely see marriages that are otherwise healthy and happy marriages but for the infidelity.

Ned Bates, a longtime Atlanta family law attorney, noted that when an affair is brought out into the open there are only two positions that are ever taken. The person who was involved in the affair says: "If everything were all right at home, I would never have gotten involved with a third party." The other spouse inevitably says: "Things were not perfect at home but they would have been okay if he/she had not gotten involved with a third party."

If you are reading this and you had an affair during your marriage, I imagine that you are shaking your head in agreement. However, if you have suffered the hurt and lack of trust caused by infidelity, you are probably wondering whether or not your bookstore would accept a return based on the fact that you didn't agree with the content of the book. Before you go searching for your receipt, please read on because truly understanding the role infidelity plays in divorce is important.

Marna Tucker, a dynamic longtime divorce attorney working in the Washington, D.C. area had this to say about affairs, "No one in a marriage goes out looking for an affair. Affairs result from a certain dynamic—someone at work they see all the time, or a neighbor they see all the time. It is so rare that someone sees a gorgeous thing at a cocktail party from across the room and says, 'Do you want to have an affair?'

"The draw of an affair is the intensity of a commonality of interest in something. Also, an affair has a wonderful unreal quality. No one says to his or her lover, 'Do you mind stopping for a quart of milk on the way over?' You drop into your lover's apartment, and she is wearing a lovely Victoria's Secret nightgown. Meanwhile, your wife is home with three young kids wearing a bathrobe over her sweatshirt because it works. Affairs are not realistic relationships."

Lori and Bob

Lori is the kind of woman that men notice. Dark straight hair frames a face with huge brown eyes and movie star white teeth. She is incredibly petite despite having had two children. Yet, her first marriage ended when she learned of her husband's infidelity.

When Lori and Bob married they were 25 and 28 respectively. They met in medical school and dated two years before tying the knot. Thanks to landing jobs as residents in two different cities, the couple only lived together for one year during their entire relationship.

Lori was wary about the physical distance that marked much of their relationship, but Bob was adamant that their marriage could work in spite of the geographical challenges.

Lori explained it this way. "I really wished I realized the difficulties in maintaining a long distance marriage before I said, 'I do.' Just one friend seemed concerned; our family and other friends did not say a word.

"Apparently, Bob could not handle the challenge of being in a marriage where he only saw his wife monthly although we spoke on the phone constantly.

"When I finished my residency, I closed up my apartment, packed my car, and drove across the country to move in with Bob. I had hardly walked in the front door when he informed me that he was in love with someone else. To say I was shocked would be an understatement. Bob never hinted on the telephone or during our monthly visits that he was involved with someone else or that he was unhappy in any way.

"I was surprised at my reaction to his confession. I was extremely forgiving. I remember telling him that 'we can get through this.' But as they say, it takes two to tango, and I was the only one dancing. Bob would not go to therapy, and even though we were now living together, he would leave evidence around our house that he was still involved with the other woman."

The benefit of time and a second marriage has allowed Lori to realize that her husband's infidelity was the catalyst for the divorce but not the cause of it. "My husband thought he could handle the challenges of a long distance marriage. If we had been living together during our marriage, I think things would have turned out differently."

Interesting Fact: So what happens to the other woman or other man? Anecdotal evidence suggests that the adulterer and his or her lover frequently do not ultimately end up getting married. Ron Rosenfeld, a Beverly Hills divorce lawyer, told me that in his experience the unfaithful spouse frequently does not end up marrying the "liberator" because that person is looked down upon by the ex-spouse and the kids.

The Exception That Proves The Rule: Although nearly every one of the 100 attorneys that I interviewed felt that in most cases infidelity was precipitated by problems in the marriages, some attorneys did note that there were a small minority of otherwise happily married spouses who cheated simply because they could. According to Atlanta attorney Ned Bates, these spouses feel that as long as their spouse is not aware of the extramarital relationship, it does not constitute a marriage threatening activity. Bates said this type of adulterous spouse tends to compartmentalize the affair.

The Internet And Affairs

"It is much easier to meet people because of the internet. Without question, the ability to obtain emotional intimacy with a stranger in a brief amount of time allows people not to seek the same with their spouse." Marshal Willick, Las Vegas, NV

"The negative effect of the internet on marriages is tremendous. The kids of the parents discover their fathers and mothers screwing around. I have had spouses busting into computers and finding all this incriminating material. People who use the internet to conduct other relationships feel safe in an unsafe medium." Norman Sheresky, New York, NY

"People who are involved in chat rooms are very vulnerable to the seduction that comes from somebody who says the right things." Lawrence Stotter, San Francisco, CA

An attorney practicing in Georgia told me about one of his recent cases that demonstrated one of the many ways that the internet has facilitated adultery. The attorney's client suspected that her husband's sudden interest in staying up late "to work on the computer" was suspicious considering it corresponded with a decline in the couple's sex life. She told her husband that she was going to sleep and the husband told her he just wanted to finish up on the computer and that he would be right up. When her husband still had not joined her in bed after an hour, she quietly walked downstairs and opened the door to his office. She was not prepared for what she saw. Her husband was sitting in front of the computer aroused and naked with a video camera pointed at the spot where his underwear should have been. On the computer screen was a live naked video of his internet "girlfriend."

Apparently, the internet has made affairs so easy that you can cheat without ever having to leave the sanctity of your home office.

Although virtual sex may not be a common use of the internet, there is no question that recent changes in technology have made affairs very easy to start and even easier to conduct. Ten years ago, if you wanted to have an affair, you would actually have to meet a person in an ordinary place like work or the gym. (Most philanderers wouldn't risk a singles bar for fear of being caught.) Your telephone access was limited. Home telephone numbers were off limits of course, and even work phones were questionable where a nosy secretary or receptionist might get suspicious of a frequent personal caller. Now fast-forward ten years. The ubiquity of the internet and cell phones have combined to make affairs not only easy to start but even easier to maintain.

Internet dating sites like eharmony.com and match.com are not only surfed by singles looking to make a love connection but also by married people who would never risk visiting a singles bar. Internet chat rooms are also a popular way to "meet" a significant other. Digital pictures are downloaded, suggestive emails are exchanged, and meetings are arranged over the cell phone. Divorce lawyers are hearing more and more about personal relationships that began in a chat room, progressed to email, moved to telephone conversations and finally ended up in a hotel room.

Atlanta attorney Elizabeth Lindsay told me about a case where a woman met a man on the internet, left her husband and two young children and flew to Seattle to be with her new love although she had never seen him in person. Many other attorneys told me about clients who started an affair or rekindled an old relationship with someone that they connected with online.

Cure It

The divorce lawyers that I interviewed told me that in about twenty five to forty percent of their cases, they were aware of infidelity by one spouse or the other or both. Still, the attorneys were nearly unanimous that in most cases of serious infidelity (by that I mean that there was both an emotional and a sexual relationship between the adulterous spouse and the other man or woman), the infidelity was precipitated by other problems in the marriage.

Atlanta attorney Martin Huddleston summed up the relationship between infidelity and divorce when he said, "Affairs are not therapeutic to a marriage." No matter what the marital problem is, an affair is not going to fix it. With that said, the real issue becomes whether or not divorce is inevitable after an affair. According to the divorce lawyers that I spoke to, an affair does not necessarily spell the end of the marriage. For the marriage to continue, and recover, three things need to happen.

First, the adulterous spouse needs to make a commitment to the marriage. He or she needs to do whatever it takes to regain the trust that was lost.

Second, both spouses need to figure out why there was an affair in the first place. The cheating spouse needs to be able to articulate what they were seeking elsewhere. Some affairs are a reaction to low-sex and no-sex marriages. But many affairs have little to do with sex. Sometimes affairs have to do with a search for love, attention, or connection that they are not experiencing in their marriage.

Finally, the victim spouse has to at some point be able to get over the affair and resume the marriage. Problems frequently arise when the hurt spouse ostensibly goes on with the marriage but never lets the cheating spouse forget about the affair. Many attorneys mentioned that they have handled cases where an affair has been over for many years but the victim spouse was never able to put the affair behind them.

OTHER RESOURCES
Books
NOT "Just Friends": Rebuilding Trust and Recovering Your Sanity After Infidelity
By Shirley Glass, Jean Coppock Staeheli, Free Press, 2004

After the Affair: Healing the Pain and Rebuilding Trust When A Partner Has Been Unfaithful
By Janis Abrahms Spring, Ph.D, HarperCollins, 1996

Websites

www.dearpeggy.com (run by Peggy Vaughan author of *The Monogamy Myth* and coordinator of a national support group called Beyond Affairs Network (BAN)

www.marriagebuilders.com

Sexual Secrets

"We have had several cases where the husband is secretly a cross-dresser." Carla Stern, Atlanta, GA

If you are living with a sexual secret in your marriage, you are far from alone. Many couples that appear to the outside world to have "normal" sex lives, have anything but. One attorney who practiced in the "conservative" South, told me about a nice suburban couple who finally ended up divorced when the woman's husband, who had enjoyed wearing women's clothing while they were making love, decided that he no longer wanted to be a man wearing women's clothing. His wife's initial relief turned to dread when he confessed that he wanted to be a woman wearing women's clothing. Although the wife, an active PTA mom and accomplished businesswoman, had tolerated her husband's cross-dressing in the bedroom, she quickly ended the marriage when her husband informed her that he had already consulted a doctor about obtaining a sex change operation.

Another attorney practicing in Beverly Hills thought he had heard it all until his attractive female client told him that the reason she was seeking a divorce was because she could no longer live with her husband's sexual secret. Apparently, the woman's husband could only perform sexually after he boiled his wife's dirty stockings, and drank the boiled water (presumably once the water had cooled).

While divorce lawyers have always known the impact that unique sexual tastes can have on a marriage, television has only recently begun to mirror what has gone on behind closed doors for years. On the top-rated ABC television show *Desperate Housewives*, Bree, a perfectionist homemaker who makes Martha Stewart seem like an amateur, discovers that her upper middle class country-club going husband has a dark sexual secret. It seems that her husband's arousal is contingent on receiving pain at the hands of his sexual partner. Too ashamed to share his sexual proclivity with his wife, Bree's husband turns to a married woman in his neighborhood who, when not baking cookies, indulges male fantasies for cash. In a scene that a few years ago could only be found on cable, Bree's husband is shown "enjoying" his mistress walking on his back with stilettos sharp enough to pop a balloon.

And in the popular HBO show *Sex In The City*, hardly a week went by without a relationship ending as a result of a new boyfriend's unique sexual proclivity. (Men who wore dog collars, were addicted to porn, or begged to be urinated on to name just a few).

Aaron and Cathy's marriage could have fit into many different chapters in this book. However, I think it fits best in this section because it demonstrates how sexual differences can affect a marriage where one of the partners decides that he or she can no longer abide by a distinctive sexual practice. In Aaron and Cathy's case, both partners initially agreed to keeping a sexually "open marriage." Ultimately, Aaron decided that he was no longer comfortable with the idea and that, combined with other problems in their marriage, spelled the demise of their relationship.

Aaron and Cathy

The marriage began routinely enough. Aaron and Cathy met in college, moved in together, and married. They were confident that the combination of their many mutual interests and a deep desire to avoid the divorce bug that had afflicted both of their parents' marriages would divorce-proof their young marriage. They never imagined that their initial agreement to keep an "open" marriage would ultimately be the nail in their marital coffin.

Aaron explained it this way. "After we married, Cathy went on to pursue her graduate degree while I continued with my undergraduate program. Almost from the beginning, both of us were more focused on schoolwork than each other. Before we got married, we agreed that monogamy was a nice idea in theory but unrealistic in practice. We decided that life is never certain and we would deal with relationships with other people if and when they developed. We mistakenly thought that affairs wouldn't really matter if the marriage had a strong basis otherwise.

"The infidelity started almost immediately on both sides. For me, I found women who were interested in my same field of study and I felt very connected to them. Although I only had sex with two of them, I had relationships with many more that ranged from connecting intellectually, to kissing and other things. My wife, on the other hand, seemed to enjoy physical relationships with many different men. We knew about each other's relationships at first; it was all very open. At some point I started feeling uncomfortable with the way our relationship was going—we seemed to be putting more time and energy into school and our other relationships than each other. I told Cathy that it was time we take our marriage seriously. She seemed to agree, but then I caught her in several lies concerning relationships with other men that she had claimed she ended.

"Meanwhile, our own sex life was near extinction. We rarely had sex. Cathy told me that for her sex was only physical and not connected with love. This applied not just to her lovers but to me as well and that really bothered me.

"Basically, affair sex was a lot more interesting to Cathy than married sex. She was only turned on to sex with me when she knew I was also sleeping with someone else. Some of the people we started hanging out with were other open relationship people. It wasn't my thing but Cathy was really into it.

"I began to feel trapped by the relationship, and we went to therapy but it was too late. While I was spilling my guts to the therapist, Cathy spent the entire time in tears and was never able to open up. Still, I did not want to get divorced.

"September 11th was a big eye opener for me. It made me realize that life could end at any moment and that it is important to be in a positive relationship. My marriage was very negative. Not only did we have sexual issues but my wife was not supportive of my career. My current wife is supportive of my career and I now realize that it is a huge factor in the success of my second marriage.

"Getting divorced was probably the hardest decision that I have made in my life. Being alone after we separated was tough. It was a hard transition but I feel I grew tremendously as a result. Basically, a lot of our marital problems came from the early infidelities and Cathy's lies surrounding them. After that, I was never able to get the trust back. My infidelity didn't bother Cathy in the same way."

The Internet and Pornography

"The new thing is the issue of spouses using pornography online. It is an addiction when your sexual obsession with pornography interferes with your relationship. The problem comes when the internet pornography satisfies your sexual desire, and you no longer want to participate sexually with your mate." Janet George, Seattle, WA

"I have seen all kinds of men viewing pornography on the internet--old shriveled men, preachers, successful businessmen. The wife doesn't understand it. She feels like 'You can choose to have sex with me anytime but you choose to do that.' It is very upsetting to many wives." Herndon Inge, Mobile, AL

"I handled a case where the wife claimed that her husband was hooked on internet pornography. Once the husband became fixated on internet pornography he stopped communicating with his wife and stopped having sex with her. The wife felt that although her husband may not have been physically straying, he was emotionally straying." Steven Lane, New Orleans, LA

Several years ago, MSNBC conducted an online survey asking people about their relationship with online pornography. Nearly two-thirds of the respondents were married (47%) or in a committed relationship (17%). Eight percent of the respondents were considered "heavy" users of internet pornography spending more than eleven hours a week online viewing pornography. Perhaps the most interesting finding from the survey is that three-fourths of the respondents conceded that they "hid from others" the time they spent online involved in sexual pursuits. One in 10 adult internet users admitted to being addicted to internet sex, and an incredible one out of seven hours of internet usage is thought to be devoted to sexual activity.

Given these statistics, it is hardly surprising that more and more divorce attorneys are hearing from their clients that their husband's internet pornography addiction destroyed their marriage. (I asked, but not a single attorney had a case where a husband was disturbed by his wife's interest in internet pornography).

Pornography, of course, is nothing new. But no longer does a man whose wife does not approve of pornography have to hide magazines, conceal X-rated videos, or sneak into topless bars. Pornography is now available on the internet for free 24/7. Today the only requirement for access to pornography is an ability to work a computer.

Cindy was devastated when she learned about her husband's seeming addiction to internet pornography. A devout Christian, Cindy believes that viewing pornography is a breach of the marital commitment.

Cindy and Kevin

"Kevin and I grew up together in a pretty small town in the Midwest. Everyone pretty much knew everyone. It seemed like nearly everyone went to your church, or your school, or both. Even if you didn't know someone personally, you still knew about them.

"Kevin and I used to see each other at church and would kind of check each other out. Friends introduced us and the rest as they say was history. We dated two years and got married. In addition to our religion, one of the things Kevin and I had in common was a desire to leave our town and move to a bigger city, which we did right after the wedding.

"We pretty much popped out two babies a year and a half apart right after the honeymoon. We waited to our wedding night to have sex because that was how we both were raised and it never occurred to me that having sex with me wouldn't be enough to satisfy Kevin.

"We were married just about five years and I thought everything was going great when I started to notice that Kevin was spending more and more time on his computer. Whenever I walked by the computer it looked like he was just checking out cars, or looking for good deals on Ebay, or checking his work email.

"It got to the point though where I would go up to bed and ask Kevin to come up with me, and he would say he just needed to do a few more things on the computer. Pretty soon I would fall asleep and I would not even know when he came up. He would just be there next to me in the morning.

"We started to argue about how much time he spent on the computer, and he would get very defensive. I talked to a couple of girlfriends about the situation, and they thought that he could be having an affair with someone online or looking at pornography. At first, I thought that was totally ridiculous but the more I thought about how strange Kevin's behavior had been and about how our sex life had really changed, I thought that maybe my friends could be right.

"My friends showed me how to pull up all the websites that were visited and how to check his email account. When he went to work the next day, I checked his email and found nothing suspicious. Just the usual work stuff, and I was really relieved. But when I went to look at the internet sites that he had visited, I was completely shocked. I had never seen anything like that in my life. A lot of things with lesbians and some of what I saw was really violent.

"I was absolutely hysterical. When Kevin came home, I absolutely flipped out and told him to get out of the house. He begged me to forgive him, which I ultimately did, but I knew I could not stay married to someone who broke our vows like that."

The Key Points

- It is very common for someone initiating a divorce not to have had sexual intercourse with a spouse for over a year.
- Infidelity is usually a symptom of other marital problems.
- Marriages can recover from infidelity when the cheating spouse renews his or commitment to the marriage, both spouses understand why the infidelity occurred and the victim spouse is ultimately able to continue with the marriage without continuing to dwell on the affair.
- Sexual secrets can destroy a marriage where one spouse doesn't approve of the sexual secret.
- Addictions to internet pornography are an increasing cause of divorce.

TWO
DIVORCE SYMPTOM #2:
UNREALISTIC EXPECTATIONS

"People go into the marriage thinking, 'After I'm married my wife will bring me my slippers the moment I get home from work,' or, 'My husband will make me breakfast in bed every day.' Most short marriages end due to these types of unrealized and unrealistic expectations."
Lewis Kapner, West Palm Beach, FL

"We have a higher divorce rate now because there is an expectation that our spouse should meet all of our needs and that they should change to meet our needs. When you get past the pie in the sky ideas of marriage, you can have a happy marriage."
Sharon Corbitt, Tulsa, OK

❖

Suzie Thorn, a family law expert practicing in San Francisco, maintains that every divorce stems from a failure of expectations. Samantha marries Joe expecting that he will make a certain amount of money so that she can stay home with the children. He doesn't. Howard marries Lynn with the expectation that their honeymoon-like passion will never diminish. It does. Anne thinks that Marty will stop getting high after he becomes a father. He doesn't.

When one or both spouse's preconceived notions about their marital future are not met, the marriage frequently fails. The problem, of course, is that many of these preconceived expectations are not realistic in the first place.

Consider the case of Mary and John, told to me by Andy Leinoff, an attorney who handles high profile divorce cases in Miami, Florida. Their case is a perfect example of the death of a marriage caused by a mutual failure of expectations.

A beautiful woman walked into Leinoff's office and told him that her husband wanted a divorce. Mary, his client, was absolutely baffled by her husband's decision to end their marriage. She told Leinoff that she was the perfect wife. She cooked, cleaned, had the body of a centerfold, and was great in bed.

Given this woman's description of her wifely attributes, the lawyer was equally mystified as to why her husband would want a divorce. Curiosity drove him to ask opposing counsel why Mary's husband wanted to end their marriage. Mary's husband's attorney said that his client complained that the couple never had sex and that his wife rarely cooked or cleaned.

As it turned out, their marriage was nothing more than a classic case of conflicting expectations and perceptions. The couple was in fact having sex once a week. The husband, who expected to have sex every night in new and exciting positions, considered weekly sex "never." The wife, who expected to have sex only occasionally, considered weekly sex "always." The wife cooked dinner twice a week; her husband had expected nightly, home-cooked gourmet dinners.

When Carl, a successful money manager, described his failed marriage to me, I immediately recognized it as a classic case of failed expectations. In his case, Carl fell victim to one of the most common of all unattainable expectations: that the act of marriage will magically transform the negative characteristics of one's spouse.

Carl and Julie

Carl and Julie met in college. Looking back, Carl realized that he had serious doubts about their relationship from the beginning.

"Julie was insanely jealous from day one. After we would go out with another couple, Julie would accuse me of being interested in my friend's wife, or of flirting with other women. All of our fights had to do with her jealousies. It got to the point where we could hardly go out in public without her falsely accusing me of checking out or flirting with other women.

"I figured that her insecurities about our relationship were caused by the fact that we weren't married. I assumed that if we were married and she knew that I was committed to her, that her jealousies would subside."

Carl and Julie's marriage was only hours old when Carl first realized that his expectation—that marriage would be the antidote to his wife's jealousy—was shattered.

"During our honeymoon, as we were checking into the hotel, we met another newly married couple who were also checking in. The moment we were back in our room Julie started accused me of checking out the wife in that other couple. I knew then and there that the marriage was not going to eliminate Julie's chronic jealousy."

The marriage limped along for another couple of years. Double dates with Carl's closest friend were off limits because Julie felt insecure about his friend's attractive wife. Counseling failed because although the therapist felt that Julie needed to be treated alone for her insecurities, she refused to acknowledge that she had a problem.

"I made a big mistake by making excuses for Julie's behavior while we were dating. I should never have expected her to change," Carl said.

A Shift In Marital Expectations

"People enter into marriages with expectations that are very high, but with a lack of ability to adjust their expectations to reality." Stephen Arnold, Birmingham, AL

Stephanie Coontz in her recent book, "Marriage, A History," notes that since the dawn of civilization, the major point of marriage was to get in-laws. Of course, today many people lament the fact that marriage comes with in-laws at all. But now that the goal of marriage is not to acquire a rich, powerful set of in-laws, what is the goal? That too has changed dramatically since the turn of the last century.

Mike McCurley is a well-known family law attorney who practices in Dallas, Texas. He thinks that to truly understand the correlation between our changing expectations of marriage and our high divorce rate, we need to understand how much the role of the husband and the role of the wife have changed. We had a long conversation about the subject. I have paraphrased here some of what he had to say:

"There has been a major social transition in America between the time my grandparents got married and today. Most of the transition has been healthy, but transition is painful.

"At this moment in history, men and woman are at an uneasy peace about their roles in their relationships; there is an uneasy balance of power as the roles of men and woman are changing. The best way to understand the change is to understand what used to be. Two generations ago, men and women had clear-cut marital roles, and the expectations of each person's role in the marriage was clear. The man's job was to take care of the business and make the money, and the woman's role was to take care of the family. The husband, without question, was the head of the family and made the major decisions.

"The men and women in the next generation still had defined roles, but they were less certain. The husband was still primarily responsible for bringing home the bacon, and the wife for cooking it up in (and washing) the pan, but now the husband may have been called on to pick up the bacon at the market on his way home from work.

"For today's spouses, much of the expectations of what a wife does and what a husband does are interchangeable. Consider the typical family where the wife works, the husband works, and there are two children. Suddenly, there needs to be a division of power. Who does what? Who has the say so over what? Nannies can do so much, but they can only do so much. Who takes what job? What friends do you spend time with? Who's relig going to follow? There is no longer a clear cut leader and follower. In tc world there are now two people who are leading."

Now that both spouses are capable of bringing home the bacon, cooking it, and feeding it to the kids, things have gotten more complicated. In addition to all of the confusion that our changing roles have created, our expectations about other things have changed as well.

There was a time where the number one trait that a wife would look for in a husband was a good provider. This is no longer enough for most women. It seems that a lot of young single women also expect their husband to look like Brad Pitt. A University of California at Berkeley study compared husband "wish lists" compiled by women in 1958 and 1998. In 1958, less than a third of women polled rated attractiveness as important; forty years later seventy five percent of women said an attractive partner was essential. But both groups said that a man's ability to earn a living was important. The study's authors concluded that women want a partner who is "attractive, ambitious, successful, sensitive and understanding."

And what about the guys? It seems that their expectations haven't changed as dramatically as women's expectations. According to psychiatrist and author Frank Pittman, "Women can actually work up some real heavy dissatisfaction and leave a marriage because of a poor guy's failure to live up to her romantic fantasies. Pittman claims that men expect less: "Men like to eat well, have sex, ...and like a wife who is not mad at them." But what they want most of all, according to the divorce lawyers that I interviewed, is the doting, carefree wife that they took with them on their honeymoon.

Unrealistic marital expectations tend to fall into one of the following categories: "marriage to anyone is better than being single," "we will always be in romantic love every day," "marriage will change my partner/marriage won't change my partner," "love conquers all." Let's take a look at the first common unrealistic expectation: marriage to anyone is better than being single.

Unrealistic Expectation #1:
Marriage To Anyone is Better Than Being Single

"When you get married it should be to be married to someone in particular."
Marshal Willick, Las Vegas, NV

"People get married for the wrong reasons. Frequently people get married just to get out of the house, or because their peers are getting married." Kenneth Koopersmith, Garden City, NY

Hanging on my computer monitor is a newspaper comic strip that sums up the confusion that some people seem to have between a wedding and a marriage. Two men are hanging out at a bar drinking a beer. One bears a huge grin and tells the other, "The wedding is off. We discovered all we both wanted was really just a big party with all our friends." The recipient of this news replies, "Excellent."

Marshal Willick, a longtime Las Vegas family law attorney, noted that there is a lot of defective reasoning as to why people get married in the first place. So entrenched is the idea that marriage automatically leads to a happily ever after that he hears comments like, "We were drinking and it sounded like a good idea at the time." Willick noted that some women get married just because they have an expectation that marriage is automatically preferable to being single. Such expectations are quickly shattered when the woman realizes that it does matter whom you are exchanging rings with.

Willick told me, "Some woman just want to get married, period. This is a bad attitude. When you get married it should be to be married to someone in particular."

Unrealistic Expectation #2:
We Will Always Be in Romantic Love.

"When people marry they believe in the fairy tale. They get so wrapped up in the fairy tale that when they find that their spouse has shortcomings, that they didn't marry a prince or princess, they think the fairy tale is still out there somewhere, and they start looking again." John Schilling, Newport Beach, CA

We all love the story of Romeo and Juliet. But Romeo and Juliet type portrayals of romantic love have really done a number on us as a society. Now we all expect to feel the type of love and passion that Romeo and Juliet felt, every single day, and over the course of an entire lifetime. (Not to mention, what was Romeo and Juliet's life expectancy at that time, thirty-five?)

But what if Romeo and Juliet hadn't died? What if they had gone on to have sleepless nights with infants, teenager induced anxiety attacks, or the stress caused when Romeo's job moved to China just before college tuition was due for the little Montague-Capulets. With all due respect to Shakespeare, if his main characters had lived, his play might have included a "Wherefore art thou workaholic husband? I have been stuck in the castle with three kids all day!"

People who go into marriage with the fantasy that they will be in romantic bliss every moment of every day for a lifetime are the ones who have the most difficult time when their romantic bubble bursts. Boston area attorney Karen Tosh described these unrealistic romantics as "love junkies."

Chicago attorney Don Schiller mostly represents CEOs, wealthy athletes, and well-known politicians. But his clients' great wealth and power do not immunize them from believing in the fiction that marriage is all about passion. Schiller told me that, "Many people incorrectly assume that the relationship will feel as good after a few years as it did at the beginning. But attraction fades, and when that change occurs the couple needs to get down to the other things that keep a marriage together. Some people only think about the passion, and mistakenly assume that is what marriage is and should be."

Schiller's observation has been confirmed by sociological research. Ted Huston, a professor of human ecology and psychology at the University of Texas at Austin, conducted a study to see if there were factors present at the two-year period of a marriage that would forecast if the marriage would last. One thing he found was that couples whose marriage began with extreme romantic bliss were particularly divorce-prone because that type of intensity is impossible to maintain.

According to an article that appeared in the *Los Angeles Times* titled "Can Success in Marriage Be Predicted?" that discussed Dr. Huston's study, the couples that were most vulnerable to disillusionment had brief courtships. "In a whirlwind romance, it's easy to paint an unrealistically rosy picture of the relationship that can't be sustained. And while all married couples eventually lose a bit of the honeymoon euphoria…those who remain married don't consider this a crushing blow, but rather a natural transition from romantic relationship to working partnership."

Those who do not make the natural transition from romantic euphoria to working partnership typically end up frustrated and bored. Sheldon Mitchell, a longtime divorce attorney in Phoenix, Arizona thinks, "The number one cause of divorce in younger people is boredom, which is not what they expected from marriage. Once people get bored with each other, they turn to other distractions like alcohol, drugs, or other men or women."

Unrealistic Expectation #3:
Marriage Will Change/Won't Change My Spouse

"The current hit play, "I Love You, You're Perfect, Now Change" puts into the popular culture what a new spouse should not be doing if they want to have a successful marriage. What you see is what you get. People do not change." Daniel J. Jaffe, Beverly Hills, CA

"If you expect all things to be the same before the marriage, as after, someone is not going to be happy." Jerry Nissenbaum, Boston, MA

Many divorce attorneys cited "marriage will change my spouse" as a common unrealistic expectation that frequently leads to divorce. Marriage and motherhood will stop her drinking; the responsibility of a wife and children will make him ambitious. Magicians can turn doves into rabbits, but the priest, minister, or judge that performs the marriage ceremony doesn't have the power to change essential attributes of the bride and groom. Nonetheless, people frequently go into marriage with the expectation that the very act of marriage will somehow transform their spouse.

Pamela Paul wrote a book called *The Starter Marriage and the Future of Matrimony* after she began to notice that she was not alone in having a first marriage in her twenties that fell apart after just a few years. She cites unrealistic expectations of marriage by her peer group as one of the reasons that these short "starter marriages" are common among twenty something and early thirty-something-year-olds. (They are "starter" marriages because these couples get divorced before they have children and go on to marry someone else.)

Paul said one woman admitted, "I suppose subconsciously I thought marriage would bring us closer together." A young man explained, "Sex was always lousy, but I assumed it would get better once we married."

I heard many of the same types of comments from the divorced people that I interviewed for this book. Many of the people that shared the stories of their broken marriages told me that before the wedding they saw the specific quality in their spouse that ultimately was responsible for the dissolution of the marriage, but, like Carl with the extremely jealous wife, mistakenly assumed that marriage would "cure" their spouse of their undesirable traits.

An equally unrealistic expectation is the corollary to the marriage will change my spouse rule. Some people enter marriage wrongly assuming that their spouse will never change. Miami family law attorney Corie Goldblum mentioned that she has witnessed several divorces that were initiated by men who couldn't deal with the fact that their wife's appearance had changed from their wedding day.

Unrealistic Expectation #4:
Love Conquers All: Different Goals and Values Don't Matter

"Did you expect marriage to be a symphony or a high school band? If both expected a symphony, or both expected a high school band, then everything is great. But if one expected a symphony, and one expected a high school band, then you have problems."
Ned Bates, Atlanta, GA

People frequently get engaged without discussing whether their life plans, and whether their values correspond with the life values or goals of their spouse. Instead, they fall victim to assuming that because they have love, they have everything else necessary to make a marriage work.

Starter Marriage author Pamela Paul repeatedly found that couples who had brief marriages had given absolutely no thought to whether or not they had common goals and values. "Many of the couples I interviewed hadn't given any thought to how marriage would fit into their own long-term goals as individuals, let alone whether or how their spouse would accommodate them. They often didn't even bother bringing up children, finances, home ownership or location—these things just seemed too removed from their reality at the time."

When you read about how incompatible goals and values frequently lead to divorce in Chapter 8, Growing Apart, you can see why the false expectation that love conquers all is dangerous to a long-lasting marriage.

Are Your Marital Problems Caused By Unrealistic Expectations?

Review the following list to see if your marital expectations are realistic or unrealistic. This list is particularly helpful for those who are single and contemplating marriage. If you are contemplating remarriage, review the list below and also read Chapter 7, Spouse Clones, Steps and The Ex.

Some Unrealistic Expectations:

- My spouse did drugs before we married, but will give them up when we have children.
- My spouse drank heavily before we married, but will "grow out of it."
- Our sex life will be just as it was on our honeymoon.
- I am not a happy person but my spouse will make me happy.
- If I nag my spouse enough, they will change.
- My spouse's appearance will never change.
- I'm not going to have sex with my spouse but my spouse will continue to be faithful.

- Children will not change our lifestyle that much.
- Women: I will change my spouse.
- Men: My spouse will never change (unless I change, and then she will change too).

Some Realistic Expectations:

- I will not suffer verbal or physical abuse at the hands of my spouse.
- Teenagers will probably put stress on our marriage.
- At some point in our marriage, my spouse and I may have to go to counseling.
- My spouse and I will probably change in some ways throughout our marriage.
- We will make financial decisions together that affect us both.
- For our marriage to work, we need to make time for just each other.
- Some days my spouse will bore me.
- Sometimes my spouse will do things that will make me angry.
- My spouse will have opinions that I don't agree with.
- I may have in-laws in my life that I don't care for.
- Our sex life might be great, but it will not be like it was on our honeymoon (or when we were single).

The simple act of knowing that a marital expectation is unrealistic goes a long way in letting go of that idealistic expectation. Once the expectation is gone, much of the resentment that was tied up with that expectation not being met tends to evaporate. Many people also have successfully changed their expectations with marital therapy, and have gone on to have happy marriages.

The Key Points

- Unrealistic expectations ruin many marriages. Marital therapy can go a long way in helping couples realize which marital expectations are realistic and which ones are not.

- Four common false expectations are:
  - We will always be in romantic love.
  - Love conquers all. Marriage can survive without common goals and values.
  - Marriage will change my spouse.
  - Being married to anyone is better than not being married at all.

THREE
DIVORCE SYMPTOM #3: **MONEY**

"The amount of money a couple has doesn't change the basic reasons that people get divorced. Whether the family income is $75,000 a year or $750,000 doesn't make a difference. It is all about the way the couple relates to money."
Ike Vanden Eykel, Dallas, TX

Long before I opened the file on my first family law case, I had heard that money problems were a leading cause of divorce. I had always just assumed that the connection between money and divorce was basically a problem for those with insufficient means. If you have a big house, a fancy car, a fulltime housekeeper, and a divorce decree with your name on it, then your marital problems must have been something other than money, right? Wrong. Even very wealthy couples are not immune to the money issues that plague marriages. The following story about the divorce of basketball legend Kobe Bryant's in-laws illustrates one of the many different ways that money issues can wreck havoc in a marriage.

Fifteen months after young and beautiful Vanessa Laine, a girl from a working class family, married Los Angeles Laker superstar Kobe Bryant, Vanessa's mother divorced her husband ending their twelve-year marriage. Vanessa's mother blamed another woman, but her ex-husband attributed the breakup to the effect Kobe's great wealth had on the couple's marriage.

The *Los Angeles Times* reported their problems this way: "Steve Laine

[Vanessa's stepfather] says that as Kobe and Vanessa lavished [Vanessa's mother] with gifts—a house full of furniture, a Mercedes-Benz S-500, $120,000 in cash, payment of phone, dental and credit card bills, payoff of their mortgage—he began to fear his wife's respect for him was crumbling.

"Vanessa's stepgrandfather…put it this way: 'All of a sudden, it wasn't "What does Steve want for dinner?" It was, "What does Kobe want?"' According to Laine, the couple's marriage ended because as a result of Kobe's wealth, he had become 'insignificant.'"

The truth is that the role money plays in a marriage is extremely complex. It brings out differences in values, it creates control issues, it touches on entrenched feelings about gender roles, and it highlights differences between savers and spenders. Most of our attitudes about money are etched into us during our childhoods and are very difficult to change.

Some people do split because of tensions created by a combination of too little money and too many expenses, but that tends to be the exception. It seems that the biggest money problems—the real marriage breakers—have more to do with the couple's money dynamic than the amount of zeros that appear on their bank account statement. In fact, most divorce attorneys will tell you that their business tends to slow down during severe recessions when money is in short supply. When a couple's marriage falls apart over money issues, it is usually because:

- There has been a significant increase or decrease in the family's financial fortunes (think lottery tickets, dot.com crashes, major career changes).
- One spouse is controlling the couple's money.
- One spouse is a "spender" and the other spouse is a "saver."
- The couple's values over where money should be spent are diametrically opposed.
- One spouse has a gambling addiction.

Let's take a look at these issues one at a time. The first step toward ending the money conflicts in your relationship is to identify the specific money dynamic in your marriage. The second step is to take aggressive action against the unhealthy money dynamic and cure your marriage of this significant symptom of divorce before it is too late.

The Catastrophe of the Financial Roller Coaster:

"A wife tells her husband, 'I won the lottery, so go back your bag!' The thrilled husband replies: 'Should I pack for cold or hot weather?' 'I don't care,' says the wife, 'just be out of here by 5:00.'" Irwin Buter, Los Angeles, CA

I came across an article the other day written by Mitch Albom, the writer who did pretty well with a book called *Tuesdays With Morrie*. He was commenting on the dramatic effect that winning a lottery jackpot appears to have on marriage. Here is some of what he had to say: "Suddenly, it seems, the belief that you can be taken care of by a windfall of money trumps the belief that you need a husband—or a wife—for your happiness. Suddenly, men envision a carefree life of younger women and endless parties, and women envision a life unburdened by the fat slob they've been putting up with for years." Money may not buy you love but it sure makes it a lot easier to leave when that love is over.

The reverse of a sudden increase in a couple's assets—a sudden and dramatic decrease—is also a major marriage buster. It is one thing for a couple to live with a finite but consistent amount of financial resources. It is another thing entirely to have had a terrific lifestyle and then have to give it back.

The reason for a large upswing or significant downswing in a couple's income doesn't always matter. It can be a lottery windfall, the sale of a successful business or invention, the loss of a job, or a major stock loss. It is the change that the sudden success or failure brings to the marriage that seems to be the challenge. Emily "Sandy" Behr, an attorney practicing in Atlanta, Georgia summed it up like this, "Where the couple's financial picture changes dramatically—they make or lose a lot of money really fast—it can break apart a marriage that is already cracked." And, even in strong marriages, financial roller coasters can make their own cracks.

Candy and Scott's marriage is a perfect example of how financial highs and lows are a lot harder on a marriage than a smooth financial ride. When Candy first told me the story of her difficult marriage, I immediately thought about something Los Angeles divorce attorney Ron Rosenfeld told me about the effect that huge financial swings have on a married couple. He said, "Money is an overwhelming catalyst for divorce when someone loses their station in life." Candy's husband, Scott, "lost his station in life" many times during their fifteen year marriage. That, and the couple's inability to effectively communicate about their finances, ultimately destroyed their marriage.

Candy and Scott:

"Scott was one of the first people that I met when I moved to New York in 1985. I was 23 and he was 28, and Scott had recently gone through a divorce. When we first met it felt like we had a lot in common. He was a talented artist, but he also owned a small business that seemed quite successful and more than paid the bills. I had previously been attracted to sort of spontaneous, aggressive artistic types who were not necessarily very stable. Scott seemed the opposite of that. He was a good guy; smart, well educated and responsible. And we seemed to have similar values and outlooks.

"When we met I was very interested in writing, and I wanted to pursue a career as an editor. I knew that writers and editors didn't do well financially at the beginning and felt that Scott's seemingly stable business and responsible nature would allow me to pursue that dream.

"A couple of year's after we married, business conditions deteriorated and his business went through a tough time, and we had just had a baby. Scott purchased everything that I asked for and hired a nanny so that I could continue to pursue my career. He never told me that we couldn't afford the things that we were spending money on. It was only after I stumbled upon our credit card statements that I discovered we were $50,000 in debt. Although Scott was a hard worker, he was in a high level of denial about our financial situation. I took a second part-time job to try to help with the situation but it didn't make much of a dent.

"Meanwhile, we went into therapy because it was obvious that we had real communication problems. I am a very communicative person and from the beginning of our relationship felt that there was a lack of connection caused by Scott's inability to share his thoughts. Although I noticed the problem from the early days of our relationship, my feeling that Scott was a good choice caused me to ignore the fact that he withdrew whenever I tried to discuss problems.

"When I learned of the way Scott handled, or should I say didn't handle, the financial problems in his business and our marriage, the entire balance of power in our relationship shifted. I always got the feeling that Scott liked having the power in the relationship and being the one to take care of things. That all changed when the financial problems started. I took charge, because I felt like he was ineffective. I think that shift in power was the beginning of the end.

"Our cash flow problems continued for years. Scott had to close up his business, and ultimately got another job. But I never felt that the new job was secure and unfortunately my instincts proved to be right.

"While Scott was having these career ups and downs, my career was going well. I became an editor of a magazine and had quadrupled my initial salary. I felt very empowered but I was also very resentful of the fact that I had to work so hard to provide financial stability for our family, and that I had little time to pursue my writing, and for my daughter.

"During this time there was a lot of animosity between Scott and me. We were constantly fighting about money and our sex life had become practically nonexistent. Scott had become very depressed during this time about the whole situation. No doubt his depression was caused in part by his losing his role as a reliable provider.

"When we finally split up, Scott started taking counseling seriously. Before that, he had gone with me on occasion but it was not effective because he really didn't want to be there. It was too late for me. At that point I had given up on him and the marriage but I think it was good for him."

You can see from Candy's comments that living on a financial roller coaster ultimately destroyed her marriage. The balance of power in their relationship shifted almost entirely to Candy, a shift that neither of them wanted. Candy started resenting Scott for his role in their financial problems and she also stopped trusting him because he initially hid their financial situation from her. Once Scott was stripped of his role as family provider, he became depressed. Not an ideal state of mind to be in when you are trying to revive your career.

Symptoms of a financial roller coaster

Do you and your spouse live on a financial roller coaster? See if any of the following scenarios sound like your marriage. Can you relate to some of the following statements?

- Have you or your spouse obtained a substantial inheritance or gift?
- Have you or your spouse had a sudden increase in income as a result of your or your spouse's career?
- Have you or your spouse had significant gambling or lottery wins?
- Have you or your spouse sold a business or invention for a large sum of money?
- Have you or your spouse ever been out of work for a significant amount of time?
- Have you or your spouse experienced a substantial business reversal?
- Have you or your spouse sustained major investment losses?
- Do you and your spouse have frequent arguments about who was/is responsible for your financial highs and lows?
- Do you feel like your financial picture is more "feast or famine" than consistent?

The Financial Odd Couple: Spenders vs. Savers

"Fights about money cause many divorces. One party wants to spend and the other party wants to save." Bob Nachshin, Santa Monica, CA

Financial guru and best selling author Suze Orman is very familiar with the money arguments that arise when financial odd couples tie the knot. She summed up the problem this way: "Couples often know everything else about one another, but have no idea what kind of 'money person' their husband or wife really is. Optimally, a couple would develop financial intimacy before making a commitment, because fantasizing about playing financial house is very different from actually doing it."

Orman's comment about not knowing how a spouse relates to money until sometime after the wedding cake is cut, applied to Sally when she married George. Although Sally knew that George was "tight" with money when they were dating, she incorrectly assumed it was because he was a business school student who was paying his own way through graduate school. Sally soon learned that she had jumped to the wrong conclusion.

Sally and George were married for twenty-five years before Sally finally filed for divorce. She told me that only the first few years of her long marriage could be called "good." Like nearly every marriage that didn't make it, theirs could fit easily into other chapters in this book. In addition to vastly different views toward money, poor communication was a marital culprit. However, because most of their fights had to do with money, I am including their story here. As you read their story, note how both Sally and George's views on money were shaped in their childhood. This is very typical.

Sally and George:

"When I left Chicago for Los Angeles in 1960, I was 22 and single. At that time, I was already considered 'old;' nearly all of my friends were married or engaged, and many of them already had children. I was thrilled when a friend's husband said he had a lot of 'boys' for me at the business school he was attending.

"George, one of the business school boys, and I really hit it off. We dated for two years before we got married. We had a lot in common. We both loved visiting art museums and traveling, and our religious beliefs were the same. I was very impressed with him at first. He seemed very worldly compared to me because he was a few years older, and he just seemed to know how to take care of everything and did.

"We did what you were supposed to do back then. George went to work, and I had three babies in four years and took care of the house. But I still remember crying as I was folding diapers because even though I had three beautiful children and a home with the latest appliances, I felt very lonely and unfulfilled.

"Neither of us had great communication skills, but a common source of friction had to do with money. George was extremely tight and could only spend money on things that were on sale or that he could bargain for. He was so concerned about spending money that he wanted me to buy the kids' clothes two sizes larger so that they could grow into them. We had money. George was successful financially. It just pained him to spend any of it. George would pay all the bills. My only role was to look over the credit card bill to make sure that it was correct.

"I love nice things and really enjoy shopping, especially for gifts. When I did buy clothes for me, I made sure that the item had been significantly marked down. I remember hanging anything new that I bought on the closet door before I put it away so that George could see from the tag that the item was on sale. He rarely would permit expenditures for new furniture and the like.

"One of the biggest problems for me was that George couldn't buy gifts (because that would entail spending money) and he had a difficult time receiving gifts from me. He returned 99% of what I bought for him so I finally stopped buying him gifts. This was very difficult for me because giving thoughtful gifts is a major way that I express love. George knew that returning the gifts hurt me but he continued to do it. I understood why he did it—he was more comfortable having the money than the gift—but it still hurt.

"I remember a time that our family took a trip, and a vendor took a picture of us. The price, and I still remember this, was just $3.00. George tried to bargain the guy down. Inside I felt like he was cheapening our entire family. I felt the same way when he bought me a gold necklace once for my birthday. He had asked me what I wanted and we went to a wholesale jewelry store to pick it up. Once we got there he tried to bargain the salesperson down even more. It felt like he was bargaining me. It was like I wasn't even worth the wholesale price. I was so upset by the experience that I didn't wear that necklace for years.

"I think that George's frugalness came from his mother. George's mother never got over the trauma of the Great Depression and was afraid to spend a dime. She stopped giving George birthday gifts when he was six years old because she did not want to spend the money. She even hid money from her husband.

"I inherited most of my money attitudes from my father. My father always seemed to have plenty of money and was happy to spend it or lend it. But my mother was a lot like George. Once my father bought my mother a mink coat and she exchanged it for a few other less expensive items. Whenever George and I fought about money, which was constantly, my mother always took his side. 'George is right! What do you need wool carpet for? Nylon is so much cheaper!'

"Even though we had major problems, neither of us thought about going for counseling or seeking help. It wasn't until we were married for more than twenty years that a friend finally suggested that we see a marriage counselor. I'm sorry that we waited so long. There was just too much water under the bridge by the time we got help. We were experts by that time at pushing each other's buttons.

"When I look back I see that we didn't really hear each other. And I bear my share of the responsibility for the divorce. I remember that George used to grow beautiful flowers in the yard and cut them and leave them in the house for me. I never appreciated that. I wish I did."

Sally and George's story shows the classic "spender/saver" marriage in action. Twenty years of resentment could have been avoided had the couple worked out their differences with a therapist early on in their marriage.

There is a large middle ground between excessive spenders on the one hand, and excessive savers on the other. Most people find themselves somewhere in this large middle ground. The issues that create problems in marriages arise when one spouse is an excessive spender or saver. (While two excessive savers could probably live happily ever after at least where money is concerned, a marriage of excessive spenders probably couldn't make it unless the couple's financial statement looked like that of Bill Gates). Read the following symptoms of "The Financial Odd Couple." Does it sound like your marriage?

Symptoms: The Financial Odd Couple
Characteristics of Excessive Savers:
- Excessive savers have a difficult time making a purchase unless they know that they received the absolute best price or the item is marked down.
- Excessive savers know precisely where all of their money goes.
- Excessive savers do not like to shop.
- Excessive savers do not give gifts beyond what is absolutely required.
- Excessive savers express concern about being poor.
- Excessive savers constantly worry about having money for the future.
- Excessive savers know precisely how much money they have in savings and checking accounts.
- Excessive savers typically grew up in a family where spending money was frowned upon, although sometimes excessive saving is a reaction to feeling financially insecure as a child.
- Excessive savers will inconvenience themselves to save money, e.g. they will drive several miles past a convenient gas station because a farther one has a minimally better price.

Characteristics of Excessive Spenders:

- Excessive spenders may not balance their checking account or know how much money is in a savings account.
- Excessive spenders shop constantly.
- Excessive spenders tend to be generous with others, e.g. picking up lunch or drink tabs.
- Excessive spenders don't typically plan for major expenses.
- Excessive spenders don't spend a lot of time thinking about money.
- Excessive spenders frequently grow up in families where at least one parent was also a major spender, although sometimes excessive spending is the result of growing up in a family with little money.
- Excessive spenders may have problems with their credit rating.
- Excessive spenders live paycheck to paycheck.
- Excessive spenders tend to be optimistic about their future income.
- Excessive spenders frequently find themselves in substantial debt.

Like someone who feels a need to unilaterally control the family finances, most excessive spenders and savers need outside assistance to help them with the relationship problems that are caused by their monetary habits. People with spending or saving issues usually never leave their spending patterns behind completely, but with help they can frequently moderate them.

Interesting Fact: Many of the family law experts that I spoke to handle what are referred to in the divorce biz as "high-end" divorces. Translated, that means they represent people who have a mind-boggling amount of money. Yet even the ultra rich can have money problems when their spending becomes "excessive" in relation to their assets. Private jets, second homes, a household staff, high-end cars and philanthropic donations can all put a strain on even healthy budgets. Beverly Hills attorney Bruce Clemens told me that very few people, no matter how wealthy, feel like they have a surplus of money.

Up and Coming Symptom of Divorce: A few attorneys mentioned to me that they are beginning to see the start of a new divorce trend. More and more highly successful women are seeking divorces from husbands who don't financially cut it. Seattle attorney Mary Wechsler mentioned that over the last few years, she has noticed an increase in cases where the "woman is unhappy about supporting a man where the man is not working or doing his share financially." Denise Mills, a Denver family law expert, noted "men are culturally used to supporting woman so that it is not an issue. But it is for many women." Mills said that she also saw a disturbing side effect to this trend; husbands who feel financially insignificant often get depressed or turn to drugs or alcohol.

Control and The Golden Rule

"Money is all about the Golden Rule: the person who makes the gold, makes the rules." Jacqueline Whisnant, Newport Beach, CA

"Oftentimes men control the money and woman control the sex. If you are mad and you are a woman, you withhold sex. If you are mad and you are a man, you withhold money." Janet George, Seattle, WA

"It is not uncommon for one or the other party to be completely in the dark about the family finances." David Walther, Santa Fe, NM

Although from a legal standpoint, money earned during a marriage (usually) belongs to both parties equally, in reality many wage earners frequently control the marital funds. Chicago attorney James Feldman explained how this type of controlling behavior damages a marriage: "When there is monetary inequality in a relationship, it feels like one spouse is oppressing the other. The other spouse is kept on a short leash and not given equal say in how finances are handled. Implicit in this is an unspoken statement from the controlling spouse that the other spouse is not competent to handle financial issues."

As irony goes, this symptom of divorce takes the cake. If the controlling spouse had not monopolized the money, he or she could have continued to have a large say in how the family money was spent. Instead, what happens is the controlled spouse finally throws up their hands and files for divorce, causing the controlling spouse to lose all control of a portion of the couple's money. After the divorce, the controlling spouse is frequently in a position of writing monthly spousal and child support checks, and he or she has no say how that money is spent. Plus, generally about half of the marital assets are required to go to the controlled spouse who will then be free to manage those assets without interference from his or her spouse.

Janet George, a Seattle divorce attorney and former marriage and family counselor, told me the ultimate money control story. She had represented the wife of a tremendous businessman and negotiator who had a habit of leaving his wonderful compromising skills at the office each night. His first marriage had broken up because he had a heavy hand when his wife spent money, while he had no problems spending money himself. His second wife complained to her attorney that when she climbed into the passenger seat of her husband's Ferrari wearing a new $40.00 sweater, he would inevitably comment that she didn't "need" the sweater. As a result of the couple's divorce, this man's second wife had less money from a purely theoretical perspective but more money from a truly practical standpoint.

Financial secrecy and control played a huge role in the destruction of Karen's marriage. Although she did have affairs toward the end of her marriage, I think that after you read her story you will agree with me that the money control virus had already infected her marriage long before she started having affairs.

Karen and Tim

Karen was 20 when she met 18-year-old Tim at a college fraternity party. Even though both were drunk when they met, Tim somehow kept hold of the scrap of paper with Karen's barely legible telephone number and Karen actually remembered who he was when he called. They quickly became college sweethearts and started planning a future together. But their future turned out not to be what Karen had anticipated.

"Growing up, my family always had financial problems. My dad was very controlling and would dictate who my mother could socialize with and try to monopolize her attention. He was not a good provider and did not work hard. In my head, I knew I wanted someone exactly the opposite of my father.

"Tim seemed the opposite of my father in everyway. He worked hard, even in college, and always seemed to have money. He was very social and outgoing unlike my father. I was not looking for love. I was looking for a man who would be a good father, financially successful, and a good husband. Tim seemed like he would fulfill each of my three requirements. The fact that I did not love him was not at all relevant to me because I could fall in love with the guy who pumped my gas but that would not get me the secure family life that I craved. I assumed if a guy who was right on paper came along that I would fall in love with him after we were married.

"Our financial problems began shortly after we were engaged. Tim wanted to invest in a business and asked me if I knew where he could get several thousand dollars to put in. Because I believed in him, I asked my grandmother if she would lend Tim the money. Even though she was not wealthy, she agreed to loan him the money because she trusted my judgment and believed me when I told her that the loan would be repaid in 90 days.

"Soon after my grandmother provided Tim with the money, the owners of the business locked him out. To this day I have no idea what happened. We temporarily called off the wedding but I did not break off the relationship. I felt like Tim was making the best of a bad situation. He was working hard at another job and we were living together.

"After we got married, Tim had a series of jobs. He absolutely controlled the money and was very secretive about it. Frequently, I had no idea where he was working, and I knew that he was always trying to juggle our finances. He was always the only one who knew what was going on and there was no talking to him about our financial situation. When I tried to talk to him, he would say everything was 'fine.' I would say, 'How is my spending?' 'Fine.' 'Can we afford to move?' 'No.' 'Can I get a new car?' 'Yes.'

"From the outside everything always looked good. Although we never owned a house, we lived in a nice rented condominium in an upper middle class neighborhood. Soon we had two girls, and I was able to buy all of the things that went with that. We sent them to an expensive private nursery school and they had the "right" clothes. But we never had adult conversations about money. Everything boiled down to power struggles. I would come off sounding nasty right off the bat because the financial situation was always frustrating.

"Hindsight is twenty-twenty, and now I see a lot of what was happening was partly my fault. I didn't look over our tax returns. I'm sure subconsciously I wanted to be in the dark.

"The happiest and saddest point of our marriage revolved around a house. I found a beautiful house in a great neighborhood, and Tim said we could afford to buy it. But the purchase fell through and we ended up renting it instead. I didn't care because my girls were so happy there. They had friends in every house on the block and spent the day running back and forth between our house and their friends' houses. It was truly a happy, happy, happy home. Tim said I should pick out things for the new house, and when the kids were in school I went shopping for furniture, plants, and the like.

"I was so content in that house that I told Tim that if my three priorities—private school for the kids, staying in that wonderful house, and being a stay at home mom—were met, that I would stop bugging him about the other issues in our marriage.

"We were not even in the house for six months when everything fell apart. Tim came home one day and told me we were broke and in debt. He said we would have to sell everything that we owned and move out of the house immediately. He told me that I would need to get a job and that we would need to borrow money from friends. At that moment I knew that the façade that I had tried to create had come to an end. Our life was like one of those movie sets. Everything looked all right from the front but when you looked in the back there was nothing there.

"The single most devastating day of my life was when we had to move. It represented the complete failure of the vision that I had for my marriage and for my kids. And I also knew that I was responsible to some extent because I had acquiesced to letting Tim control our money and our spending right from the start of our marriage.

"We moved into a small rental house and I became very depressed. I spent more and more time on the internet and even joined some dating sites. I know this sounds crazy, but I started to date just like when I was single. Because I was barely secretive about it, Tim found out. When he confronted me about the affairs, I had absolutely no emotion. We were never bonded or connected like a husband and wife so I did not feel the slightest bit guilty. He was part of my family but he was not like my husband. We were never a team.

"I think Tim was surprised about the affairs because our sex life had been so bad. He had always wanted it and I always tried to avoid him. Because I had never wanted *him,* he mistakenly assumed that I just never wanted sex, which wasn't the case.

"Even though Tim said he would take me back, I knew that I could not go back into a situation where Tim was responsible for our financial future. I realized that it had now fallen to me to make sure that our girls always had a place to live, food and clothing. So I rented my own place and went to work.

"My financial situation is better now because I am working and know how much money is coming in, when it is coming in, and how it is being spent. But my personal relief about money anxieties is continually metered and measured against my children's discomfort with the divorce. They deserved none of this. Even though Tim and I attend all school and family functions together and don't fight, I think that my kids will probably end up on a shrink's couch because of the divorce. One day I will have the devil to discuss this with.

"What should I have done differently? I should have chosen to be a strong woman earlier on. I think I should have not been so blind and should have put my foot down. I should have left the marriage before starting other relationships. Tim did what he did but it was my fault because I allowed those things to happen to me. I lived on a hope and a prayer that things would change on their own and that was stupid."

I really don't need to add anything to Karen's story because she did an excellent job of summing up what she should have done differently. Clearly, if this couple had sought help for the dysfunctional way that they handled money early on in their marriage, much of what transpired could have been avoided.

Karen is not alone in living in a marriage with financial blinders on. I heard over and over again from the divorce attorneys that I spoke with that women frequently come in for a divorce without any understanding of their finances. They don't know how much their mortgage is, they don't know if they have savings accounts or retirement accounts, and they have no idea how much their spouse earns a year.

Do you have unilateral control of the money in your marriage? Review the following symptoms of a typical controller.

You probably have too much unilateral control over the family finances if:

- You unilaterally make all or nearly all of the major financial decisions.
- You do not permit your spouse to have access to checking and saving accounts that contain money that legally belongs to both of you.
- You hide money from your spouse.
- You keep your spouse in the dark about how much you earn.
- You do not allow your spouse to see bills and credit card statements.
- You closely monitor how much your spouse spends on even small items.
- You insist that you and your spouse file separate tax returns even if there is no financial benefit to filing separate returns.
- You file joint tax returns but you do not let your spouse review the return before signing it.

- Your spouse frequently complains that they do not feel like they have any control over your joint finances.

Do you feel like your spouse has too much unilateral control over your joint finances? If you can relate to many of the following statements, your perception is probably correct.

Your spouse probably has too much unilateral control over the family finances if:

- You have no idea how much your spouse earns.
- You do not have access to any money that you can spend freely.
- You never see checking account statements, savings account balances, stock market account statements or credit card statements.
- You have no idea how much your mortgage payment is.
- You do not know how much (if any) life insurance you have.
- When you ask your spouse questions about your financial situation, he or she is evasive.
- Your spouse does not let you (or you don't) review your tax returns before signing them.
- You and your spouse almost never discuss your short term and long term financial goals.
- Your spouse dismisses your requests to be involved in financial matters.

If you review these symptoms and conclude that you or your spouse has too much unilateral control over your joint money, you must take immediate steps to remedy the situation. This is not something that can be swept under the rug for another year, or two, or ten because there is no doubt that money control issues cause divorce.

If you find that you are unable to fix this problem on your own (or if the controlling spouse refuses to acknowledge the problem), then you absolutely must find a qualified therapist to help you resolve the problem. Doing nothing on this one is not an option.

Don't Show Me the Money. Show Me the Values.

In chapter 8, I discuss the relationship between vastly different values and divorce. Differences in how people feel money should be spent could certainly fit into that section. Still, I wanted to share Allison and Howard's story with you now because it shows how even when both spouses feel like they have joint control over the family money, are similar in terms of spending and saving philosophies, and haven't had any major highs or lows in their financial life together, differing values about where money should be spent can still cause major problems in a marriage.

Allison and Howard

Allison and Howard's marriage did not end in divorce thanks to the help of a very good, pro-marriage therapist. But for a while, it looked like they had a divorce lawyer in their future.

When Allison and Howard married, Allison was a third grade teacher at a private secular elementary school, and Howard was a principal at a local high school. Even before their wedding, they had agreed upon a financial plan. They would both work for six years before they had children in order to save for a down payment on a house. Once the children were born, Allison would stay home and take care of the two or three children that the couple planned on, and that is what happened. Well almost.

After the couple was married for just two years, their unplanned child was born. Allison stayed home with their daughter. Money was tight, but the couple still managed to squirrel away a small amount each month for their house fund.

Before long their daughter was attending a private nursery school. The couple diverted the monthly house fund payment to pay for school tuition. One day Howard offhandedly remarked how he was looking forward to the day when their daughter was in public school so that they could get back on track saving for a house. Allison, who had assumed all along that their daughter would attend private school and that the house was on an indefinite hold, was taken aback. She felt very strongly that their daughter attend a private elementary school. Howard felt just as strongly that she attend public school so that they could afford a home.

After World War III erupted, the couple decided to try to resolve their differences with the help of a therapist. The therapist helped them outline their choices and made some suggestions that had not occurred to either of them. Allison decided to return to teaching after their daughter was in Kindergarten to help pay the private school tuition, and to increase the money that was set aside for a house. The new plan, which worked well for them, meant that they would put off the birth of future children, perhaps indefinitely, but both Allison and Howard felt that was a necessary compromise.

How do you want to spend your money? Save it for your child's college tuition at an Ivy League school? Buy a different pair of $1,000 Manolo Blahnik shoes on the first of each month? Purchase floor seats to watch your favorite basketball team, and front row seats behind the dugout of your home baseball team?

The first step in resolving different financial dreams is to let your spouse know what those dreams are. Fill out the following short questionnaire with your spouse. You might be surprised by your spouse's responses.

Him:

For the short term, I feel like our money needs to be spent on the following things first:

_____

_____

_____.

If there is extra money in the short term, I think that it should be saved (circle) or spent on:

_____

_____

_____.

For the long term, I would like to save money for:

_____

_____

_____.

Her:

For the short term, I feel like our money needs to be spent on the following things first:

_____

_____

_____.

If there is extra money in the short term, I think that it should be saved (circle) or spent on:

_____

_____

_____.

For the long term, I would like to save money for:

_____

_____

_____.

Any surprises? The next step is to work out a financial plan that works for both spouses. Feel free to use any format that works for you. (Your local bookstore will have numerous books on creating a financial plan if you need help.) If your differences in financial values are so great that you feel that you can't devise a plan where both of your major (no one will get everything they want, so prioritize) values are met, you must seek help from a professional financial advisor or from a marriage counselor.

Interesting Fact: Does a lot of money keep people together or just make it easier for them to split? Although most attorneys will tell you that recessions keep people together because the couple recognizes that they don't have enough money to support two households, many lawyers feel that some people stay married regardless of their feelings for their spouse because while they can contemplate losing their spouse, they can't bear the thought of giving up their lifestyle. Family law attorneys Robert Boyd and Elizabeth Lindsey told me that in Atlanta, money is frequently the tie that binds. Where the money is good, women will put up with a lot to keep the kids in private school and to keep the nice house. When money gets tight, things go down hill quickly.

Gambling

"Gambling can be a major problem and can take many forms. It is not only about blackjack and slot machines. Some people are gamblers with their businesses and investments." Irwin Buter, Los Angeles, CA

"I see spouses with gambling addictions on a fairly regular basis. The non-gambling spouse is dealing with a diminishing pot and feels like he or she needs to cut their losses and get out." Ike Vanden Eykel, Dallas, TX

At the outset of this book I made it clear that not all marriages can, or should, be saved. If you are married to a compulsive gambler and he or she will not recognize the problem or submit to help, a divorce may be the only thing that can save you from eventual financial ruin.

I am including some information about Gamblers Anonymous, a self-help group for gamblers who have admitted that their gambling is out of control, in the key points at the end of this section. Unfortunately, there is no way that you can force your spouse into Gamblers Anonymous. He or she has to want to join the program for it to work

I am also including information on how you can contact Gam-Anon, a group for families and close friends of compulsive gamblers. If you feel that you are not sure whether or not your spouse's gambling is out of control, answer the following questions developed by Gam-Anon. Remember "gambling" is not limited to the horse races and the slots. People frequently gamble with money in the stock market or with risky investments. The Gam-Anon questions apply to those types of situations as well.

According to Gam-Anon, answering "yes" to at least six of the following questions means that you are living with a compulsive gambler.

1. Do you find yourself constantly bothered by bill collectors?
2. Is the person in question often away from home for long, unexplained periods of time?
3. Does this person ever lose time from work due to gambling?
4. Do you feel that this person cannot be trusted with money?
5. Does the person in question faithfully promise that he or she will stop gambling; beg, plead for another chance, yet gamble again and again?
6. Does this person ever gamble longer than he or she intended to, until the last dollar is gone?
7. Does this person immediately return to gambling to try to recover losses, or to win more?
8. Does this person ever gamble to get money to solve financial difficulties or have unrealistic expectations that gambling will bring the family material comfort and wealth?
9. Does this person borrow money to gamble with or to pay gambling debts?
10. Has this person's reputation ever suffered due to gambling, even to the extent of committing illegal acts to finance gambling?
11. Have you come to the point of hiding money needed for living expenses, knowing that you and the rest of the family may go without food and clothing if you do not?
12. Do you search this person's clothing or go through his or her wallet when the opportunity presents itself, or otherwise check on his/her activities?
13. Does the person in question hide his or her money?
14. Have you noticed a personality change in the gambler as his or her gambling progresses?

15. Does the person in question consistently lie to cover up or deny his or her gambling activities?

16. Does this person use guilt induction as a method of shifting responsibilities for his or her gambling upon you?

17. Do you attempt to anticipate this person's moods, or try to control his or her life?

18. Does this person ever suffer from remorse or depression due to gambling, sometimes to the point of self-destruction?

19. Has the gambling ever brought you to the point of threatening to break up the family unit?

20. Do you feel that your life together is a nightmare?

The Key Points:

- Remember, gambling comes in all forms. It can be taking crazy risks in the stock market, with investments, or with a business.

- If you feel like your spouse is gambling to such an extent that it substantially threatens your home and savings, you need to consult a family law attorney about how to protect your marital assets. Sometimes the smartest move is to file for divorce and obtain court orders to protect your property. If your spouse seeks help for the gambling addiction, you can put the divorce on hold while your spouse takes positive steps to bring their gambling under control.

- You can encourage your spouse (but can't make them) seek treatment for their gambling. One place to turn is Gamblers Anonymous. It has a 12 Step Program similar to Alcoholics Anonymous with support groups all over the country. Their website is www.gamblersanonymous.org and their telephone number is (213) 386-8789. There are also other treatment programs available.

- For your own personal support, contact Gam-Anon at www.gamanon.org or 718-352-1671

To Prenup or Not Prenup:

"Every marriage ends either by death or divorce." Marshal Willick, Las Vegas, NV

You can't write a book about the role that money plays in marriage and divorce without talking about prenups. "Prenup" is lawyer lingo for a prenuptial agreement, a contract that is signed before marriage, which designates how a couple's money and property will be divided if one party to the marriage should die or the couple splits up. Although it would be nice to add a few paragraphs into the agreement designating your spouse for permanent garbage can duty, prenuptial agreements are all about designating money, and property as either his, hers, or both.

Who needs a prenuptial agreement? Not just Donald Trump who recently bragged in his new book that he would never get married without one, but anybody who is entering a marriage with substantial assets. What constitutes a substantial asset? Your 1991 Toyota Corolla may have loads of sentimental value, but it is not the type of property that needs to be protected by a prenuptial agreement. If you are going into a marriage and own a Toyota dealership, a prenuptial agreement is probably in order. Ditto for couples who are entering marriages with significant holdings in retirement plans, stocks, bonds or other investments, and real estate.

What do prenuptial agreements do? To understand how a prenuptial agreement functions, you first need to understand how the law concerning marital property rights works. Before you get married, every dime that you earn and everything that you own belongs to you and Uncle Sam. When you get married, that all changes. (Except for the Uncle Sam part). How it changes depends somewhat on the state that you live in, but most states tend to lump all property into marital or community property on the one hand, and separate property on the other hand.

Separate property usually (and again every state has different rules) includes everything that an individual owned before they got married, and gifts and inheritances received after the marriage. Marital or community property usually includes most everything that is acquired by either spouse after the priest, rabbi, or justice of the peace deems a couple "husband and wife."

I think the best way to show how prenuptial agreements affect the legal status quo is with a hypothetical. Let's take Elizabeth Taylor's marriage to her eighth husband, construction worker Larry Fortensky. All of Liz's premarital assets, things that were hers before she married Larry, like money that she earned from being a movie star and entrepreneur, houses, cars, and jewelry all belong to her. All of Larry's premarital assets belong to him. Saying "I do" and kissing the bride didn't change any of that. But things frequently become less clear-cut when additional money or property is attained after the marriage, and that is why people with substantial pre-marital assets like Elizabeth Taylor usually follow their attorney's advise and enter into a prenuptial agreement before sending out the wedding invitations.

Now imagine that since their fabulous wedding, Larry and Liz have been very busy eating in the best restaurants and taking exotic trips in Liz's private jet. When they are in town, Larry spends his time driving back and forth to Home Depot in Liz's Rolls Royce for contractor's supplies that he is using to update her mansion. He purchased the supplies with the money that he earned when he sold his own small home to move in with Liz.

Liz has been spending most of her time since their wedding chatting with Michael Jackson, raising money for AIDS research, and writing thank you notes for the very expensive gifts that the couple received. She also spent a couple of weeks shooting print ads for the many perfume lines that bear her signature.

Suppose that on the couple's first wedding anniversary, two envelopes arrived in Liz and Larry's mailbox. The first envelope contained a residual check for $250,000 for movies that Liz made thirty years ago. (They were recently rebroadcast on cable.) The other envelope contained a check for $1,000,000, which was issued from the company that manufactures the many fragrance lines that Liz promotes. The pay stub on the check clearly states that the money is for fragrance sales that occurred over the past year.

Under California law, and the law of most states, the residual check would be Liz's separate property. Assuming that she put it directly in an account marked "separate property," Larry would not have a legal leg to stand on if he were to make a claim to that money. But what about the money from the perfume sales?

If the couple got divorced, Liz would argue that the money was hers. The perfume lines were created long before she met Larry, and people presumably were persuaded to buy that perfume because of the reputation Liz had made for herself no thanks to Larry. Larry would claim that the money was half his because Liz used marital time to market the perfume when she shot the print ads. And if Liz put the perfume money in a joint account, Larry would have further ammunition for his claim.

Let's add one more wrinkle to our hypothetical. Liz and Larry call their respective divorce attorneys sometime after their fifth wedding anniversary. Larry claims that the house doubled in value thanks to his remodel, and that he is entitled to half of the increase. He also claims that he is entitled to a million dollars a year in spousal support because now he is accustomed to dining in high-end restaurants, drinking fine wines, and wearing designer clothes. Eating at McDonald's and wearing Levi's are now out of the question. Oh, and the limited edition Rolls Royce that Larry drove regularly was obviously a "gift" from Liz, because she always referred to it as "your" car, as in "Larry, honey, let's take your car."

The point of prenuptial agreements is to put an end to these types of expensive and time-consuming squabbles by deciding *before* the marriage how any property that comes into the marriage after the wedding will be divided upon divorce. If Larry and Liz had a prenuptial agreement, all of the issues with respect to the increase in value of the house, the money from the perfume sales, and the residual checks for her old movies should have been addressed.

Honeymoon brochures, wedding dresses and engagement rings are romantic. Prenuptial agreements are not. In fact, many would be marriages never happen because of the fights and hard feelings caused when prenuptial agreements are negotiated. But that is not a bad thing.

The reason that prenuptial agreements break up potential marriages is because the conversations that prenuptial agreements force on couples weed out people who do not have compatible ideas about money. And, as you have already learned, people who aren't on the same money page frequently divorce. On the other hand, once you have gone through the process of negotiating a prenup, your expectations of how money will be handled tend to be very realistic. One attorney, Phyllis Bossin, who practices in Cincinnati, Ohio, told me that she has had clients tell her that negotiating their prenuptial agreement prevented many arguments down the road because it forced them to discuss money issues before exchanging vows.

When people negotiate a prenuptial agreement with a prospective spouse, they learn:

- Exactly how much money their fiancé earns and what real and personal property they own. This is no small thing. Many people don't have a clear idea of what their significant other earns and owns until after the wedding bells have rung. (And even then, some people don't find out!)
- About their future spouse's expectations concerning how "family" money will be handled. Parties to a prenuptial agreement quickly learn if their intended has visions of keeping most of his or her money "separate" or placing all of their earnings together in a joint account. And, for the spouse who is initiating the prenuptial agreement because he or she has significant assets, he or she will quickly learn what their spouse's expectations are concerning those assets.
- Whether their potential spouse tends to be a saver. Prenuptial agreements don't always weed out major spenders, but they do tend to shine a light on people who are major savers. If you read a draft of a prenuptial agreement and learn that your potential spouse has $10 million in the bank and earns a million dollars a year, but drives a dilapidated car and only buys used

clothes, you are engaged to a major saver.

- Whether their potential spouse feels a need to control money. If your love hands you an agreement to sign that states that he or she will have exclusive control over both his or her separate property assets, and community or marital assets, take note of the large red money control flag that your man or woman is waving.

Most of the lawyers I spoke to think of prenuptial agreements as a necessary evil for anyone who either has substantial assets or is in a unique position to earn or acquire substantial assets. (Imagine someone with a rich single uncle, or a computer nerd who has spent five years developing a unique software program that is about to come to market). They are "necessary" for individuals who have substantial assets especially when that person has children from another relationship. The "evil" part is that no matter how you dress it up (I just ran across a book optimistically titled *Prenups For Lovers: A Romantic Guide To Prenuptial Agreements*), prenuptial agreements are all about divorce. It is hardly surprising that the average engaged couple would rather plan for their wedding than for their divorce. Many of the attorneys that I interviewed told me that some of their clients who had signed a prenuptial agreement resented it from the moment that they signed it up to the time that they signed the divorce papers that the prenuptial agreement anticipated. "If you loved me you would never have asked me to sign a prenuptial agreement," is a common refrain.

With that said, most attorneys do not recommend prenuptial agreements for first marriages where neither spouse has substantial assets or extremely wealthy relatives because of the resentment that they tend to cause. When I practiced law, I worked on a case where the couple had divorced after twenty years of marriage and three kids. I really liked our client. She was smart, funny, and attractive and her soon to be ex-husband seemed to be her mirror image. If it weren't for the fact that they were about to get a divorce, I would have wanted to fix the two up on a date, they seemed so perfect for each other.

I asked our client about their marital problems and she said that her husband insisted that she sign a prenuptial agreement even though at the time she married him he was just out of law school and his only "asset" was the debt from his substantial student loans. "A prenuptial agreement would not have bothered me if he had a lot of money when we married or if he had children that he wanted to protect from a prior marriage. But when we got married all that he had was a lot of potential. I had always expected that once he realized that I was committed to our marriage he would tear up the agreement. Then I thought that he would tear it up after our children were born because we were both so happily married at that time. But he never did. That prenuptial agreement ate away at me to the point that I lost feelings and respect for him. It told me that the contribution that I made to our life was meaningless and that only his financial contribution mattered."

If you are single, or if you have already gone through one divorce and are reading this book because you don't want to go through another divorce, a prenuptial agreement may be in your future. Most family law attorneys draft them. It is important to know that both you and your future spouse will need independent counsel. Your attorney will go over the basics with you, but here are a few things that you should discuss with your significant other *before you* see your attorney:

- Discuss your current, and anticipated assets. Be direct. There is no point in beating around the bush because prenuptial agreements typically contain a list of each spouse's assets as part of the agreement.
- Discuss whether or not your prenuptial agreement will ever expire or be modified. Some people feel that if they are married for a substantial amount of time, the prenuptial agreement should no longer be in effect, or that certain terms should be made more lenient.
- Talk about how you will handle day-to-day expenses like clothing, food, manicures and the like. If you think that there is a possibility that you will have children together, and it is your husband who is trying to protect his assets, have a very blunt discussion about what money would be available to

you in the event that you stopped working. (Do not assume that you are one of those people who would never want to stay home with your children! Many people who felt that way before they had children change their tune after their first child is born.)

- Discuss your attitudes about your material priorities. If you think it is important to have a home that would make the cover of *Architectural Digest* and your potential spouse appreciates a bohemian garage sale look, that is something that needs to be discussed. Same goes for the type of car that you expect to drive and how much you think is appropriate to spend on jewelry and clothing.
- If this is a second marriage, and either or both parties have children, discuss who is going to pay for college and private school tuition, and where that money is going to come from.

The Key Points:

- There are five types of money issues that typically cause divorce. They are:
- Excessive control over joint money by one spouse
- Different values as to how money should be spent
- Excessive spending or saving habits
- Extreme financial highs and lows
- Las Vegas type of gambling, making wild investments, taking unjustified business risks
- Prenuptial Agreements are recommended where one spouse has substantial assets. Most attorneys advise against prenuptial agreements where neither spouse has substantial assets to protect (or anticipates substantial assets) at the time of the marriage.

THE DIVORCE LAWYERS' GUIDE TO **STAYING MARRIED**

FOUR
DIVORCE SYMPTOM #4:
COMMUNICATION

"The definition of good communication is the effective transfer of information. For the transfer to be effective the communicator must communicate with empathy, choosing the correct tone and time, and the recipient must be receptive to receiving the information."
Steve Harhai, Denver, CO

"I'm always surprised when one client comes in and describes how awful the relationship has been and the other spouse thinks that everything is fine."
Helen Christian, Salt Lake City, UT

"Poor communication is the overriding issue in most divorce cases. It may sound like sex or money, but it really boils down to communication."
Ike Vanden Eykel, Dallas, TX

❖

Just as I was beginning my research for this book, a friend and I were communicating about communication; communication with spouses to be specific. I told my friend that I thought that this chapter on communication would be the most difficult to write because the word "communication" itself is vague. Does it mean a failure to tell your spouse what is on your mind, or a failure to really listen to your spouse? Does it have to do with what is said or how it is said? And there was something else that was troubling me. "What is confusing about the divorce symptom of communication," I said, "is that communication between the couple must have been working somewhat in the first place if the couple decided to marry. So what changed?"

It was this last question that really caught my friend's attention. She pointed out that what happens when a couple is married is that the type of information that gets exchanged changes. To make her point, she used the analogy of the patient information forms that we all fill out whenever we visit a doctor for the first time.

When we visit a new doctor, we are required to answers dozens of questions concerning our past medical history and often the medical history of our parents. This is necessary, of course, because the doctor does not know us or our backgrounds, and that information is important to the way that he or she will perform their examinations. But we really need to go through that exercise only once. After that, every year or so when we go back to that same doctor, his or her office manager will simply hand us our old form and ask if there have been any changes. Sometimes there are and sometimes there are not, but usually there is not a lot to tell. To fill out the update takes a minute or two at the most.

Similarly when we were first dating our spouses, they knew nothing about us so we had a lot of information to exchange. We shared our personal histories, stories, dreams, political views, and favorite jokes, and our spouses shared theirs. We told them about our parents, our siblings, and our friends. At some point, the major information was pretty much exchanged; after that, everything became the equivalent of "updates."

After marriage, there is a perception between spouses that there are many fewer things to tell because they have already explored the major issues. We know our spouse's favorite color, their political persuasion, and all about what they do for a living. And, we start saying things like, "Oh, I know what you are going to say." It is this unconscious perception that we have heard pretty much everything that the other person has to say that changes the way that we communicate with our spouses after we are together a few years.

The divorce lawyers that I spoke to had a lot to say about communication. While most did not mention communication as the overriding factor in marital breakdowns, a significant minority thought that three of the biggest marriage busters, money, sex problems, and growing apart, were really just communication problems in disguise.

Bill Hunnicutt, a family law expert in Denver, said, "People don't listen anymore. Spouses need to take the cotton out of their ears and put it in their mouth for a while." Minneapolis attorney Ed Winer said, "Many people get divorced because they never form that communication bridge, and they lose patience with each other. They don't spend the intellectual capital to come up with joint solutions to their problems." Sandra Morgan Little, a divorce lawyer in Albuquerque, New Mexico, said, "Communication is like an octopus with many different arms; it relates to sex problems, and money problems. Most problems relate back to communication."

I think that the most dramatic detail that I was told about marital communication problems is that many, many people had no idea that their spouse was even unhappy in their marriage let alone were privately considering divorce. Clearly there was a substantial breakdown in communication in those relationships.

Marital communication has three parts: telling, listening, and depth. When communication breaks down at any of these stages, problems occur in the marriage. Fortunately, this is one area where a little help goes a long way. However, that help needs to come *before* the resentment that bad communication causes gets out of hand. The divorce lawyers that I interviewed told me over and over again that their clients waited until the communication symptom had thoroughly infected their marriage before seeking help. By then, they were well on their way to a divorce lawyer's office.

The Problem With Telling

"Putting your spouse down in public is a serious symptom of divorce." Peter Sherman, Washington, D.C.

It seems like "telling" should be simple. If there is something on your mind, you just say it, right? But telling is actually quite tricky. It involves proper timing, a respectful tone, and a spouse who is open and receptive to what you have to say. If you hesitate to discuss important issues with your spouse, or if your spouse reacts poorly to your telling, an experienced marriage counselor can help you find a way to improve your communication style.

Stacy and James

Stacy and James had a major telling problem in their marriage. Stacy wouldn't express her feelings about things that bothered her about James and James would not tell Stacy things that bothered him until he felt ready to explode. Fortunately, one of Stacy's friends convinced her to seek counseling early in her marriage to fix both of their telling styles. The result is that after a year of working on the problem, Stacy is more open, and James has learned to communicate without a temper. Here is what Stacy said:

"I grew up in a family where there was no yelling at all. If my parents argued behind closed doors, my siblings and I didn't hear it. That was a great way to grow up because there was not a lot of overt stress. On the other hand, I don't think any of us really learned how to express ourselves in a constructive manner. The minute my brothers and sisters started to have the normal childhood arguments, my dad would step in and 'solve' the problem for us. That stopped a lot of fights but it was not helpful in letting us practice the skills necessary to work out normal disagreements.

"James grew up in a family where yelling was like talking. Everyone spoke in the same tone to each other, which was usually sarcastic, negative, or condescending. I'm sure one of the things that James liked about me was that I was always 'nice' and rarely got angry.

"I never really heard 'the tone' as we now call it when James and I were dating. Probably because we had such a short engagement, and I'm sure we spent most of that time just kissing and smiling. Plus, there isn't a lot to get upset about before you have kids, and a big mortgage really.

"After we had our first child things became very stressful. James would lose it over the smallest things. The screaming was very hard on me because I didn't grow up that way. Instead of confronting him about it, I pretty much just shut down.

"I was at a mommy and me class when our daughter was about one year, and a couple of other moms were complaining about their husbands. I mentioned that my husband had a temper problem and I didn't know how to handle it and that it was making me extremely depressed. My daughter was only one so he wasn't yelling at her yet but I knew that it was just a matter of time. One mom gave me the name of her marriage counselor. She said that I had to go right away because things would only get worse. She had the same kind of thing going on in her marriage and she said that the counseling really helped.

"I never in a million years thought that James would consider going to therapy. But that night I got a babysitter, made a dinner reservation for the two of us, and got up the courage to tell him how unhappy his negative tone and the yelling were making me. I didn't mean to start to cry, but I did. I told him that I loved him and wanted nothing more than to have a good marriage.

"I give James a lot of credit for his response. He said he really didn't know that he had been yelling that much and that the last thing he wanted was to hurt me. And he said that he wished that I had spoken up sooner. Anyways, we ended up going to that counselor and she helped us both a lot with our different communication issues. She made me see that I couldn't just clam up when things upset me and she helped James with his temper and his tone.

"James and I do not have a perfect marriage, if there is such a thing. But things are much, much better than they were."

The Problem With Listening

"How people communicate in relationships is a big issue. Every relationship requires that the parties stand up for themselves and assert themselves. How they resolve their issues determines whether they will stay married. Frequently the problem is one spouse goes underground like a submarine when communicating and that doesn't work."
James Feldman, Chicago, IL

The best way to demonstrate how challenging listening can be, is to share Allison and Andy's story with you. Both Allison and Andy had trouble listening but their listening problems manifested themselves in different ways. Andy's listening problem was that he was a "defensive" listener. Whenever Allison made a request to Andy, Andy responded defensively.

Allison: (In a neutral tone) Andy, I see you did not take out the trash. Just a reminder that tonight is trash night.

Andy: (In an angry tone) Can't you see that I have been doing homework with the kids and catching up on business calls? I'll take it out later.

Whenever Andy brought up something to talk to Allison about that she was uncomfortable discussing, she would avoid the conversation, and ignore the request.

Andy: Allison, you spend a lot of time at the gym and with your friends. I would like you to make some time for me.

Allison: Fine. (But then she would continue her gym and social routine as if Andy had never made the comment).

When I spoke to Allison about her recent divorce, she freely acknowledged that each of their communication styles contributed to their break-up. This is what she said:

Allison and Andy

Andy and Allison dated for two years before they got married. Allison told me that she did see some potential problems in their communication styles early on, but she thought "she could change some things." But after seven years of things not changing, Allison finally dragged Andy, kicking and screaming, to a therapist. It was in therapy, Allison said, that she learned that she actually did not have the power to change another person; that if they wanted to change, they would have to do it alone.

"When we were dating, I was concerned about Andy's self-centeredness. It seemed like everything needed to be his way—he had a one-way street kind of attitude. On top of that, we are both very stubborn. Even though I had concerns, we went really well together on paper. We both grew up in big cities and were the same religion. He was a successful professional so I knew that I would not have to worry about money. I was a teacher, which was fine when I was supporting myself, but I knew that I could never send kids to college on my salary.

"Most of our marital problems had to do with the fact that, in addition to being stubborn, both of us were bad communicators. We never really got to the heart of the things that were bothering us in our marriage; instead, we just kept shoving them under the rug. Over time that rug got really crowded.

"I really never felt emotionally connected to Andy. And when I would tell him that I was unhappy, and thinking of taking our two kids and leaving, he wouldn't say, 'I love you. I want this to work. Let's work out our problems.' Instead he would try to threaten me. He would say things like, 'Fine, leave if you want, but the kids will suffer and we will both end up in apartments.'

"We really just had a bad psychology between us. Whenever I brought anything up Andy would just get defensive. Frequently, I wouldn't even bother to say what was on my mind. And, I'm sure I frustrated Andy because he wanted our marriage to be the center of my life, and I pretty much found other things to do with my time to avoid him. Maybe the best example of the fact that our communication was terrible was that Andy was really surprised when I consulted with a lawyer and filed for divorce.

"I realize that I am a classic avoider. I was not a fighter. But even though I did not yell, I still maintained a very silent level of anger. We looked good in public but underneath it all, we were just two people going down different roads."

As Allison freely admitted, the way she listened to Andy was to barely acknowledge that he had made a request for a change, but not respond at all to his request. Her response could have been to have a deeper conversation about his request if she disagreed with it, or to acknowledge his request, and make some time for him, but she did neither.

The way Andy listened to Allison was to become angry and defensive whenever she made a request or wanted to discuss something about their relationship that was bothering her. Ultimately, Allison shut down rather than continue to attempt to discuss things with someone who was so clearly not receptive to hearing them.

The Problem With Depth

"People just lose interest in the other person and what the other person has to say."
Elizabeth Scheffee, Portland, ME

Communication at the start of a relationship usually is one of two types. The first type is extensive communication that feels like one is talking to a "soulmate." These couples share all of their innermost thoughts and feelings with each other and typically feel very close and connected. (Remember the patient information form analogy?)

The other way that communication manifests itself at the start of the relationship is that deep communication is not occurring, but the couple is so high on chemistry that it feels like they are communicating. Feeling in love is communication enough.

Communication begins to break down with the first group when their focus changes from each other to babies, houses, and work. Typically one spouse begins to feel less and less connected to their spouse. According to the family law experts that I spoke to, it is mostly women that complain that a breakdown in communication has left them feeling lonely or bored in their marriage. This also explains the results of a recent survey conducted by the Gallup company for the National Marriage Project at Rutgers University where 80% of the women that responded said it is was more important to have a husband who can communicate about his deepest feelings than to have a husband who makes a good living.

Communication problems occur with the second group—the group that never really communicated at all—when the intense chemistry that marks new relationships starts to fade. Of course, by the time one spouse (again usually the wife) realizes that they never really bonded with their spouse on an emotional level, there is usually a baby or two in the picture and a mortgage payment to make once a month.

This is one of those symptoms of divorce when just being aware that there is a problem is half the battle. For some people, making regular time to have intimate conversations is enough. Other couples will benefit from regular communication tune-ups with a good marital therapist.

Communication Challenge For Singles

Janet George is a Seattle based divorce attorney. Prior to becoming an attorney she did family counseling for many years. George suggested that couples contemplating marriage should engage in some communication role-playing to determine if they have the communication skills necessary for a marriage.

The trick is to come up with several scenarios that might occur in a marriage that have no clear solution. (For example, in the following hypothetical there is no outsider available to help the situation). Come up with your own impossible scenarios, but feel free to begin with the one that Janet George gave me.

Imagine that you have a two-year-old child. Wife, after looking for months, just landed her dream job, beating out five hundred other applicants and her start date is the next day. Husband, a lawyer, has a big trial that he has been working on for months which also starts tomorrow. Your poor, adorable little boy has a fever of 104 degrees, and your day care won't accept sick children, and there is no one else available to take care of the child. Discuss what you would do.

Cure It

Dallas attorney Mary McCurley mentioned that the new trend in psychology is cognitive therapy. The focus of cognitive therapy is rapid problem solving as opposed to spending weeks discussing childhood feelings. McCurley recommended that couples experiencing marital problems work with a cognitive therapist rather than a traditional therapist because it allows the couple to deal with specific problems quickly, and then move on to the future.

Many times throughout this book, I recommend that you find a good marital therapist to help you and your spouse work through specific problems. Of course, finding a top-notch marital therapist is sometimes easier said than done. Michele Weiner-Davis, MSW, is a relationship expert, seminar leader, and the author of several successful books on keeping marriages together including *The Divorce Remedy, Divorce Busting*, and *The Sex-Starved Marriage*. She was gracious enough to loan me her guidelines for choosing a marital therapist.

Michele Weiner-Davis' Advice On How To Find a Therapist

- Make sure your therapist has received specific training and is experienced in marital therapy. Too often, therapists say they do couple's therapy or marital therapy if they have two people sitting in the office. This definition of couple's therapy is ludicrous. You can't identify the type of therapy that is taking place by doing a head count. Marital therapy requires very different skills from doing individual therapy. Individual therapists usually help people identify and process feelings. They assist them in achieving personal goals.

  Couple's therapists, on the other hand, need to be skilled at helping people overcome the differences that naturally occur when two people live under the same roof. They need to know what makes marriages tick. A therapist can be very skilled as an individual therapist and be clueless about helping couples change. For this reason, don't be shy. Ask your therapist about his or her training and experience.

- Make sure your therapist is biased in the direction of helping you find solutions to your marital problems rather than helping you leave your marriage when things get rocky. Feel free to ask him or her to give you a ballpark figure about the percentage of couples he or she works with who leave with their marriages intact and are happier as a result of therapy. Although your therapist is unlikely to have a specific answer to that question, his or her reaction will speak volumes. You should end up feeling confident that your therapist's primary goal is to help you work out your problems so that you can remain together.
- You should feel comfortable and respected by your therapist; that he or she understands your perspective and feelings. It is not acceptable if your therapist sides with either you or your spouse. No one should feel ganged up on. Good marriage therapists understand both sides of the story and help couples negotiate solutions. If you aren't comfortable with something your therapist is suggesting—like setting a deadline to make a decision about your marriage—say so. If your therapist honors your feedback, that's a good sign. If not, leave.
- The therapist's own values about relationships definitely play a part in what he or she does and is interested in when working with you. Since there are few universal rules for being and staying in love, if your therapist insists that there is only one way to have a successful marriage, find another therapist.

  Also, although some people think that their therapists are able to tell when a person should stop trying to work on his or her marriage, therapists really don't have this sort of knowledge. If they say things like, "It seems that you are incompatible," or "Why are you willing to put up with this?" or "It is time to move on with your life," they are simply laying their own values on you. This is an unethical act, in my opinion.
- Make sure you (and your partner) and your therapist set concrete goals early on. If you don't, you will probably meet each week with no clear direction. Once you set goals, you should never lose sight of them. If you don't begin to see some progress or start to feel somewhat better within

two or three sessions, you should address your concern with your therapist.

- It's my belief that couples in crisis don't have the luxury to analyze how they were raised in order to find solutions to their marital problems. If your therapist is focusing on the past, suggest a future-orientation. If he or she isn't willing to take your lead, find a therapist who will.

- Know that most marital problems are solvable. Don't let your therapist tell you that change is impossible. Human beings are amazing and they are capable of doing great things—especially for people they love.

- Most of all, trust your instincts. If your therapist is helping, you'll know it. If he or she isn't, you'll know that too. Don't stay with a therapist who is just helping you tread water. Find one who will help you swim.

- Finally, the best way to find a good therapist is word-of-mouth. Satisfied customers say a lot about the kind of therapy you will receive. Although you might feel embarrassed to ask friends or family for a referral, you should consider doing it anyway. It increases the odds you'll find a therapist who will really help you and your spouse.

So don't give up on therapy, give up on bad therapy.

2005 Copyright - Michele Weiner-Davis, MSW. All rights reserved.

The Key Points:

- When a couple has serious communication problems, the best thing that they can do is work out their negative patterns with a therapist. Although there are many books on the subject that can be helpful, it is usually most beneficial to consult a therapist because it is very difficult to be objective on this issue.

    The American Academy of Matrimonial Lawyers published a pamphlet called *Making Marriage Last: A Guide to Preventing Divorce,* which has several good general tips on marital communication. They are not a substitute for marital therapy if you and your spouse have serious communication issues. However, they are good to keep in mind on a day-to-day basis. The entire list is available at www.aaml.org. However, I'm including my favorites here:

- Focus on solving the problem instead of winning the argument.
- Listen with an open mind to make sure you understand what your spouse means instead of launching into an unnecessary argument.
- Explain yourself if you feel you have been misunderstood.
- Spend time discussing problems and issues you each think are important.
- Be quick to forgive, quick to forget.
- Be sincere. Your words may say one thing, but your body language may convey something completely different.
- Don't talk in code. Say what you mean, and say it respectfully.
- Don't talk to your spouse in a rude, disparaging way or criticize your spouse in front of others.
- Don't start arguments based on things that happened long ago.

THE DIVORCE LAWYERS' GUIDE TO **STAYING MARRIED**

FIVE
DIVORCE SYMPTOM #5: **CONTROL**

"Many problems occur in a marriage when one person
wants to be the 'Power Person.'"
Elizabeth Lindsey, Atlanta, GA

❖

Allan Zerman, a family law specialist practicing in St. Louis, thinks that control issues are a serious cause of divorce because they touch on nearly every marital concern. Zerman explained that, "The struggle for control or the desire for control drives a wedge in the relationship. It may manifest itself as a kid issue, a money issue, a sex issue, or an in-law issue, but it all comes down to control. Some people are as addicted to control as they are to breathing.

"The irony is that few people recognize that the problem in their relationship has to do with control. The controller doesn't recognize the quality in him or her self. They rationalize it by saying that they are just trying to do what is best for the other person.

"A real control freak will try to isolate the other person from their friends and family. Where the problem is truly pervasive, not one friend or family member is acceptable. At some point the controlled person wakes up and then there is a divorce."

Dallas attorney Mary McCurley told me that she has had clients who are so tightly controlled that they had a difficult time "sneaking away" to come to her office for a consultation.

"Control" is not a one size fits all symptom of divorce. It manifests itself when a wife doesn't allow a husband to parent the children, when an in-law pulls financial strings, when one spouse puts down the other spouse in front of their family and friends. Verbal abuse and physical abuse are overt methods of control, but control can often be subtle. It can range from how much money is available to buy the sheets (read about money control in chapter three) to what happens between those sheets.

Although control comes in many different packages, the effects of control on the marriage are the same. The controlled spouse does not feel valued or respected. There is an uneven balance of power in the marriage and one spouse is left to feel unequal.

Generally, it is control issues between a husband and wife that are responsible for the downfall of a marriage. But that is not always the case. Control has many faces and sometimes its face looks like your mother-in-law or your father-in-law.

Control By Parents

"In-laws are one of the biggest causes of divorce. Parents won't leave their kids alone. Parents ought to take a course on how to be in-laws." Baxter Davis, Atlanta, GA

"When in-laws detect problems in the marriage and see the blood in the water, they frequently stir the pot and make reconciliation impossible." Joanne Ross Wilder, Pittsburgh, PA

The wild success of the television sitcom "Everybody Loves Raymond" was no doubt in large part attributable to Deborah's overbearing mother-in-law, Marie. Marie never missed an opportunity to meddle in every aspect of her son Ray and his wife Deborah's life. Nothing was off limits. She continually put Ray in "who do you love more, your mother or your wife?" dilemmas. She relentlessly interfered with the couple's arguments, their sex life, and their parenting decisions. Watching that show was like watching an in-law car wreck each week and it captured the attention of millions of viewers.

Although the vast majority of the attorneys that I interviewed felt that most in-laws didn't possess the power to bring down an otherwise good relationship, they did see examples of in-laws that toppled marriages built on fragile foundations. Sometimes, bad feelings toward in-laws start with the wedding when a mother-in-law puts her two (or three) cents in about who "must" be invited. And sometimes the in-law control begins just after an engagement ring is placed on a finger and mom and dad insist that their future son or daughter-in-law sign a prenuptial agreement before marrying their wealthy (or soon to be wealthy) child. After the wedding, problems occur when in-laws give gifts with strings the size of rope attached. Of course, when those strong strings are eventually pulled, the daughter-in-law or son-in-law often feel bitter and resentful.

Newport Beach, California family law attorney Philip Seastrom mentioned that it is not uncommon to find marriages weakened by overbearing parents telling their children how to raise their kids and in-laws who give their kids money for a new house but never let them forget it. "Remember, part of this house is mine," they say.

One attorney told me about a case where the father-in-law had so much control over his son and daughter-in-law's marriage that he chose the couple's house and picked his grandkids' private school. The daughter-in-law wrote her father-in-law a very reasonable letter requesting some autonomy over her marriage and her children. Her husband, who could not stand up to his father, left the marriage after his wife gave him a copy of the letter.

When you read the "Marital Advice From Divorce Attorneys" at the end of this book, note how many lawyers suggest that you thoroughly check out a potential spouse's family before proposing. That advice is based on two things. How you are raised significantly impacts who you are, and in-laws can help a marriage stay on track or derail it.

Cure It

What can you do if an in-law is causing significant marital stress? Discuss the issue with your spouse. Tell them that when issues arise between you and your in-law, you need their support. However, if the problem has less to do with your in-law and more to do with the fact that your spouse takes his or her parent's side against yours, find a good marital therapist who can help you shed that negative pattern.

Verbal Abuse

"A husband and wife will say things to each other that they wouldn't say to a stranger on the street." Marsha Elser, Miami, FL

Beverly Hills divorce attorney Bruce Clemens has seen many marriages destroyed by verbal abuse. He told me that, "Verbal abuse occurs when one spouse needs to dominate and control the other spouse and uses words to do that. The words are used to humiliate, break down or wear down the spouse so that the spouse becomes more dependent and subservient and susceptible to being dominated."

Verbal abuse is so common in divorce cases that many lawyers didn't even mention it until I asked about it. When I did ask, I might as well have asked if their clients breathed air or ate food. It was that commonplace.

Although throughout this book I try to convince you that it is far easier to fix symptoms of divorce than to face the ramifications of divorce, unfixable verbal abuse and physical abuse are exceptions to that rule. Studies show (and family law attorneys concur) that it is usually better for children of high conflict marriages to live with divorced parents than in an "intact" household.

What do I mean by *unfixable* verbal abuse? If the verbally abusive spouse is not willing to a) acknowledge the problem and b) work hard with a therapist to correct their behavior, a divorce is usually the only way to end the abuse. (Don't assume that because verbal or emotional abuse is not physical that it is not abuse. Verbal abuse can cause as much or more emotional damage than physical abuse.)

A friend of mine called me and told me that I should speak to her friend Ashley who left her verbally abusive and controlling husband eight years ago. Her call could not have been better timed as I was in the midst of writing this chapter.

Ashley and Joe

Here is Ashley's story. When you are reading it, keep in mind that Ashley is a very bright, successful woman who has an MBA and a high-powered job at a Fortune 500 company. If you are single, pay careful attention to how Ashley's husband's controlling behavior manifested itself when they were dating.

"I am 43 now, and I met my ex-husband when I was 26 years old and he was 28. We dated for nine months and got married nine months later. The things that attracted me to him were that we were both professionals, he came from what seemed like a good family, and he was honest and he seemed like he would make a good father. The decision to marry him was based more on logic than love.

"The first year of our marriage was okay. Things got difficult the second year when our twin boys arrived. Even though we were both working full time, Joe did very little to help with the kids unless you count his telling me everything I was doing that was supposedly wrong. Joe was very controlling and hypercritical. He continuously put me down. Nothing I did was ever good enough. I didn't stick up for myself because when I did, it would just escalate into a big fight. On a daily basis he would call me stupid, a slob, lazy, irresponsible, and spendthrift. It didn't matter who was in the room. He would do this in front of the kids or in front of company."

I asked Ashley what finally gave her the strength to pull the plug on the marriage.

"I had tried to leave many times but Joe always threatened me. I don't think it was necessarily me that he wanted. I think it had more to do with control and the fact that he didn't want me to take the kids. The straw that both broke the camel's back and gave me the strength to leave no matter what was when one of my little boys, who was four at the time, called me 'stupid' with the same tone that my husband used. I didn't want my children to grow up thinking that it is normal for a husband to speak to his wife the way my husband spoke to me.

"Although things didn't really hit the fan until after the kids were born, in hindsight there were a lot of signs I failed to pay attention to. For one thing, Joe's father is a very controlling man. There were also signs when we were dating that I mistook for caring and loving. To give you a silly example, when we were dating I might say, 'I am craving french fries, let's go get some.' And even though I was very thin, he would tell me that I shouldn't eat them. He would also lecture me on what clothes I should and shouldn't wear. Things of course get worse after marriage because the few filters that were there before the marriage were gone.

"I am very happy now but things were not easy after I left. When I filed for divorce, I suggested that we share custody. He said that I was a bad mother and went for sole custody. Because of his allegations and decision to seek sole custody, all four of us had to be evaluated by counselors. I was terrified that he would somehow get the boys but in the end the court awarded primary custody to me.

"As my kids got older, he started doing to them what he had done to me. Ultimately, he lost all custody because of the trauma that his verbal abuse caused to the kids and they now live with me fulltime."

When I asked Ashley if there was anything else that she wanted to add, she said this: "Toward the end of the marriage we went to a counselor, but it was pointless because my husband refused to acknowledge that he had very controlling behavior and that he was abusive. He has had a lot of trouble staying employed because of his behavior problems. Joe really needs individual counseling, not joint counseling.

"If you really want to know if you are with the right person you need to see if they fight fair and how they handle conflict. When the going is great, everything is wonderful. The real issue is when times get hard. How is your spouse going to handle those situations?"

Symptoms of a verbally abusive marriage
You are verbally abusive if:
- You are constantly criticizing your spouse.
- You call your spouse names like fat, ugly, stupid, moron.
- You frequently criticize your spouse and put your spouse down in front of others.
- You frequently use profanity when fighting with your spouse.

You are being verbally abused if:
- Your spouse constantly criticizes you.
- Your spouse calls you names like fat, ugly, stupid, moron.
- Your spouse frequently criticizes you and puts you down in front of othe people.
- Your spouse frequently uses profanity when the two of you fight.
- Your spouse makes you feel like everything that you do is wrong.
- Your spouse nearly always speaks to you with a derogatory tone.

Cure It
If your spouse refuses to get treatment for the abusive behavior and you feel like you have to leave the marriage, contact a family law attorney in your area for advice on how to protect your assets.

Physical Abuse
"The reason that it frequently takes a long time for someone who has been physically abused to leave the marriage is because it takes a long time to believe that the person you love would really hit you." Lynne Gold-Bikin, Norristown, PA

"The great misconception is that abuse is rampant only in the lower socio-economic groups. The truth is that physical abuse cuts across all social, economic, gender, and religious lines." Marshall Wolf, Cleveland, OH

Brenda was the last person who you would expect to be the victim of domestic violence. Her former husband is a highly respected doctor and she is an experienced nurse. Her three kids attended the best private school, played little league, and lived in a home in a prominent zip code. But even though Brenda is the last person you would expect to find in a hospital emergency room holding a towel under a bloody nose and an ice pack over an eye that would soon be black and blue, she is actually the best person to represent the face of domestic violence. While her situation is far from typical, it demonstrates how domestic violence can creep into any marriage under the right circumstances. It also shows how verbal abuse, drug and alcohol abuse, and domestic violence are often inextricably linked.

When you read Brenda's story you will not be surprised to learn that her husband Tony was raised by a mother who was an abusive alcoholic and that he had a less than reliable father. But how long Brenda put up with Tony's outrageous behavior might surprise you. Here is her story.

Brenda and Tony

"Tony was absolutely my first love. We met when I was in college and he was in his second year of medical school. He had been homecoming king in high school, president of his college, and was absolutely gorgeous with this fabulous body. Needless to say, he was extremely self-confident and in comparison I had very little self-esteem. He pretty much called all the shots when we were dating and I was a complete pushover. When he proposed I was absolutely thrilled. I wish I could say the same about my family.

"We hadn't even been married a year when I caught him in what would be his first, but far from his last, affair. He begged forgiveness. The therapist I was seeing at the time said that I needed to either forgive him and go forward with the marriage or end the marriage. For reasons I can't even explain, I stayed with him.

"When I was pregnant with our first child he started to have a problem with drugs. We had both been occasional recreational drug users, but I stopped completely when I was pregnant. But Tony kept using and he added alcohol to the mix.

"When my husband was high or upset with me he would become verbally abusive. He would treat me like shit and then send me flowers at work the next day. The big joke among the nurses when the flowers arrived was that he must be very guilty about something.

"The first affair was just one of many. He 'lost' three wedding rings over the course of fifteen years and at one point I was diagnosed with a sexually transmitted disease. We would fight about this, of course, and he would promise that he would never cheat again. I was so scared to live without him that I chose to believe him. Plus, I had three children at that point and was afraid to be out on my own. Looking back, I see how I was already on my own, but I didn't see that then. Fear is such a strong, strong emotion.

"I had threatened to leave him many times, and when I did he would become verbally abusive and pretend to hit me. He also told me that if I ever left him he would kill me. I think going to Al-Anon helped me find the courage to finally leave him.

"Last year, after a fifteen-year marriage, I finally told him that I had had it. He said he wanted to meet me and I said no. I had the kids in the car, and he called me on my cell about 10 times in a row but I didn't answer. When I finally answered, he said he was going to kill me. I told him not to threaten me. He said that was a promise, not a threat.

"When he came to the house, I had our three kids in the car and I was on my way to the market. He insisted on getting in the car and I let him in the passenger's side because I didn't want to upset our kids. He started yelling at me in front of the kids and telling me that I couldn't leave him. When I told him that it wasn't the appropriate time for that kind of conversation, he said you had better ★★!!%ing listen to me. And then he hit me in the face with his fist. I pulled over when I felt the blood running out of my nose.

"It was absolute chaos. The kids were screaming, 'I hate you daddy. I can't believe that you hit mommy!! I hate you! I hate you!'

"Tony had gone to AA off and on and I had always hoped that he would stick with it so that we could keep our family together. When he hit me, I think it finally sunk in that sobriety was a fantasy that was never going to happen. I had threatened Tony a million times over the years that I would leave. I finally, finally did it and I am so glad I did."

Domestic violence in our society is the elephant in the room that nobody seems to see. It is frequently concealed with sunglasses, long sleeves, and lies. None of our favorite shows have "battered spouse" episodes and girlfriends don't chat about it over lattes. But make no mistake, domestic abuse is out there. Police officers see it. Emergency room doctors see it. And divorce lawyers hear about it more frequently than you would think. Plus, there are the sad statistics.

In 2001, more than half a million American women were victims of nonfatal violence committed by an intimate partner. Domestic violence does not limit itself by race or religion. And although women are the vast majority of victims of domestic violence, women also commit domestic violence. In the year 2000, 1,247 women were murdered by a husband or boyfriend and 440 men were killed by a girlfriend or wife. For one-third of women who experience abuse, the first incident occurs during pregnancy.

Need more? A boyfriend or husband perpetrates an astonishing twenty-eight percent of all violence against women. (Bureau of Justice Statistics Special Report: National Crime Victimization Survey, Violence Against Women, January 1994). And, contrary to the rationalizations of victims, domestic violence is rarely a "one time thing." According to Bureau of Justice Statistics, during the six months following an episode of domestic violence, thirty two percent of battered women are victimized again. According to another study on the subject, nearly half of the men who beat their wives did so at least three times a year.

Eleanor Breitel Alter, a New York City matrimonial lawyer, explained that the reason that the domestic violence cycle is so awful and difficult to break is that woman who grew up in a house with domestic violence think that is what men do. And boys who grew up in those houses think that is what men do. It is very difficult to get a woman who is being physically abused to leave. She says things like, "But he promised he would never do it again" or, "I shouldn't have worn that dress, because it is too sexy."

Still, for those of us that are lucky enough never to have experienced a physically abusive relationship, it is difficult to comprehend why the victim stays. Las Vegas family law attorney Marshal Willick told me about a case that demonstrates how even bright, successful people can find it difficult to leave an abusive marriage.

Willick represented an intelligent, articulate, successful female attorney who suffered physical abuse at the hands of her attorney husband for two years before she finally sought a divorce. But there is even more to this story. The woman was a deputy district attorney whose job was prosecuting domestic violence cases.

While most of this book is dedicated to keeping marriages together, physical abuse very often warrants divorce. It is a problem that can rarely be fixed. Although there are treatment programs for the rare abuser that is willing to admit to the problem and commit to treatment for the long haul, many abusers won't take that minimum step.

And for those of you that think that you are doing your children a favor by staying married to their abusive father, consider the following letter written to a newspaper advice columnist by a woman who stayed with her abusive husband.

"Dear [Columnist]: I now see the damage I did to my adult children by remaining in an abusive marriage during their formative years. They have all been divorced—one of them twice.

"My husband was verbally, emotionally and physically abusive. I tried to be the peacemaker. However, by not standing up to him, I taught my children that they should not stand up for themselves. All of them have been verbally abused by their spouses and are still intimidated, just as I was.

"When I was a young wife, women were trapped with no place to go when abuse occurred. Now, with just one phone call to the police, action is taken. I hope someday I can forgive myself for the damage I have inflicted on my family. Is there a way I can help them now or is too late?"

Unlike the other chapters in this book that are geared toward keeping your marriage together, this chapter will teach you how to identify if you are married to an abusive spouse and, if so, how to take your marriage apart and move on with your life.

Are You Married to an Abusive Spouse?

Many women have a difficult time admitting that they are married to an abuser. (Because in the vast majority of cases the abuser is the husband, and the victim is the wife, I frequently use the work "husband" for the abuser, and "wife" for the victim. However, if in your case the reverse is true, please forgive my generalizations and take the advice that is appropriate to your situation.)

The American Bar Association Commission on Domestic Violence has defined physical domestic violence this way: "Physical violence includes putting your hands on a person against their will. It is shoving, pushing, grabbing, pulling or forcing someone to stay somewhere."

The National Domestic Violence Hotline website has a list of questions to help determine whether or not an individual is in an abusive relationship. I am reprinting their questions here because people who are tightly controlled by their spouses frequently do not have access to a computer, or their spouse strictly monitors their access.

Does your partner:
- Act extremely jealous of others who pay attention to you, or use jealousy to justify his/her actions?
- Control your finances, behavior and even whom you socialize with?
- Make you afraid by using looks, actions, and gestures like smashing things, destroying your property or displaying weapons?
- Threaten to kill you or commit suicide?

- Make all the decisions?
- Stop you from seeing or talking to friends, family or limits your outside involvement?
- Act like the abuse is no big deal, it's your fault or even deny doing it?
- Threatens to kill your pets?
- Put you down in front of other people, humiliate you, play mind games and makes you feel as if you are crazy?
- Prevent you from getting or keeping a job?
- Take your money or limit your access to the family income?
- Threaten to take the children away?

Do you:
- Become quiet when he/she is around and feel afraid of making him/her angry?
- Cancel plans at the last minute?
- Stop seeing your friends and family members, becoming more and more isolated?
- Find yourself explaining bruises to family or friends?

If you answered yes to any of these questions, you may be involved in a relationship that is physically, emotionally, or sexually abusive.

Other signs of a physically abusive relationship:
Your partner has:
- Damaged property when angry (thrown objects, punched walls, kicked doors, etc.)
- Pushed, slapped, bitten, kicked or choked you.
- Abandoned you in a dangerous or unfamiliar place.
- Scared you by driving recklessly
- Used a weapon to threaten or hurt you.
- Forced you to leave your home.

What to do:

If you are in an abusive relationship, but don't know how to leave or where to go call the National Domestic Violence Hotline at 1-800-799-7233. They have the addresses and numbers for domestic violence shelters all around the country.

Other options include calling your local police department and asking them to help you leave your home. Of course, if you feel that you are in immediate danger, you should dial 911. However, doing nothing and allowing the abuse to continue is not an option!

If you feel like you would like a divorce

One good way to find a family law attorney is to get a referral from either a friend who has gone through a divorce and was satisfied with the representation that she received, or to get a recommendation from a professional that you deal with regularly like your accountant. Unless your divorce is extremely simple (short marriages, no children, few assets to split), you should make sure that the attorney who represents you is experienced in family law specifically.

A good family law attorney will obtain restraining orders for you if your spouse has been violent in the past, and will help you protect your assets.

The website www.lawyers.com can also refer you to a lawyer in your area. Make sure that you enter "family law" under specialties. Another good source to locate a qualified family law attorney is the American Academy of Matrimonial Lawyers website at www.aaml.org.

The Key Points

- Many marriages break up because one spouse attempts to control the other spouse.
- Controlling in-laws can further damage an already difficult marriage.

- Emotional and verbal abuse is also a major symptom of divorce.
- Physical abuse warrants a separation or divorce from your spouse. The National Domestic Violence Hotline is 1-800-799-7233.

THE DIVORCE LAWYERS' GUIDE TO **STAYING MARRIED**

SIX
DIVORCE SYMPTOM #6:
MENTAL CHALLENGES AND
PHYSICAL ADDICTIONS

I was surprised by a lot of what I learned in writing this book but nothing surprised me as much as the number of divorces that are caused by a spouse's addiction to drugs or alcohol. It didn't matter if I was talking to a lawyer who divorced extremely wealthy people, older people, younger people, or people with moderate incomes. West Coast, East Coast, small town, big city attorneys all said the same thing—drug and alcohol addiction accounts for a substantial number of divorces each and every year.

Alcohol and drug abuse are discussed together for two reasons. First, they frequently go hand and hand. Many alcoholics occasionally use drugs and many drug users frequently drink. Second, the physical consequences of drug and alcohol addiction may be different but the effect on one's marriage tends to be the same.

Mental illness, mostly depression and bipolar disorders, although not as prevalent as alcohol or drug abuse, also accounts for a small but consistent part of every divorce lawyer's practice.

The good news (if you can call it that) about alcohol and drug issues, and mental illness, is that there are excellent treatment programs available to help lick these problems. Where a spouse actively pursues treatment, the marriage typically bounces back. Unfortunately, the same cannot be said for another infrequent, but tragic marriage buster—death or serious illness of a child. Although thankfully divorce lawyers don't encounter many marriages that have been devastated by a child's death, it is a factor in a small number of divorces each year.

Alcohol and Drug Abuse

"In one-third of the cases that I see there is some evidence of alcohol, illegal drug or prescription drug abuse." Maurice Kutner, Miami, FL

Two former husbands and one former wife shared their stories about how drugs and alcohol destroyed their marriages. The people I interviewed did not fit into the stereotypes that we have concerning the types of people who become addicted to drugs and alcohol. In fact, each of the three addicts portrayed below were quite successful before their addictions got the better of them. I'm including each of their stories here because each couple was primarily plagued by one of the three types of substance addictions: illegal drugs, legal prescription drugs, and alcohol.

Illegal Drugs
Helen and Kyle

Helen was born in Greece and moved to the United States with her family when she was eight years old. Eleven years later, at the innocent age of 19, she found herself in a Reno quickie marriage chapel exchanging vows with Kyle, her 25-year-old boyfriend. But she was happy.

Although the wedding may have appeared spontaneous to outsiders, Helen felt she knew Kyle well. She had first met him when she was 14, and had been involved with his best friend during her high school years.

When I interviewed Helen she was thirty-four, but it was clear that her feelings for her ex had been intense. Her first descriptions of him were all positive—he was devastatingly handsome, outgoing, and warm. He was the type of guy who "would do anything for anyone." And, Helen noted, Kyle always had tons of friends.

Prior to their marriage, Kyle "liked to party." Although both of Kyle's parents had been alcoholics, the young Helen did not feel that his drinking and cocaine use were a real problem. She learned quickly that she had been wrong.

"Kyle had a hard time holding down a job. He would have a good job as a controller for six or eight weeks and then I would eventually get a call from his employer asking why he didn't show up for work. He would party for five or six day periods where he simply wouldn't come home. During this time, I was trying to work and finish college. His frequent disappearances made this very difficult. Because I really loved him, I tried to get him help. He half-heartedly attended NA (Narcotics Anonymous) and even enrolled in a rehab program, but he was never able to give up the coke and whatever else he was abusing. He went to rehab but he never really made the commitment to give up the drugs permanently."

Finally, towards the end of what would be a five-year marriage, Kyle admitted that his drug problem was destroying the couple's relationship. But he felt like he couldn't stop. Helen summed up their problems well: "He loved me, but he loved drugs and alcohol more."

It was clear that Helen still loved her husband when she divorced him. Darla Goodwin, a Seattle based family law attorney, sees that pattern frequently with alcoholics and drug addicts. "The thing with addictions is that the person coming in for the divorce often still loves their spouse, but they feel that they have to get divorced to protect themselves financially. What makes many of these couples different is that they didn't necessarily feel that they wanted to get divorced, but they felt that they had no choice," she said.

Prescription Drug Abuse

"Although many divorces are caused by drug and/or alcohol issues, these types of problems are often the easiest types of problems to fix if the affected party is willing to seek help." Steven Lake, Chicago, IL

Chris and Lisa

Chris and Lisa met in March of 1993 through a mutual friend. Both were products of an upper middle class upbringing. Chris was an outgoing businessman and Lisa worked as a manager at a high-end retail store.

"We were 30 and 29 when we met and we just got each other. We were both very social and liked to party. But where I would have the occasional joint and enjoyed martinis, Lisa's past included an addiction to the prescription drug, Vicodin.

"When our relationship started to get serious, I told her that I was concerned about the Vicodin. She swore to me that her addiction was in the past and I tried to believe her although I saw occasional evidence that she still used the drug. We got engaged on our one-year dating anniversary. But as our wedding approached, I was less concerned with Lisa's past relationship with Vicodin and more concerned about our frequent fights and arguments about her dislike for my family and close friends. In fact, shortly after the wedding invitations were dropped off at the post office, my doubts caused me to consider calling off the wedding. But Lisa begged me not to, and asked me to forgive her behavior."

An event at the wedding would turn out to foreshadow future difficulties. Contrary to their private vow prior to the wedding not to engage in the tradition of smashing cake into each other's faces, Lisa rubbed cake all over Chris' face and into his hair. Chris was so angry that he didn't spend the night with his new wife in the hotel. And so their tumultuous ten-year marriage began.

I asked Chris why he went ahead with the wedding since he had a lingering feeling that Lisa was still taking drugs. He said "he felt like he was rescuing Lisa from being the out of control party girl." But Lisa could not, or would not, be rescued.

"Shortly after we were married, I discovered that Lisa had resumed her relationship with prescription drugs. I told her that the future of our marriage depended on her obtaining counseling and entering a rehab clinic. She did both. I told her that if she ever resumed her affair with drugs I would leave."

The birth of their first and only child in 1997 did not strengthen their relationship. They continued to have bitter fights about the amount of time that Chris devoted to his family, and friends. And Lisa accused Chris of having a gambling problem. During this fragile time in their marriage, Chris found out from a friend that Lisa had both resumed her drug use and had become involved with other men. Chris filed for divorce.

Alcohol Abuse

The story of Mike and Beth's marriage could have fit well into many places in this book. Even before their third child died of SIDS (sudden infant death syndrome) at two months of age, their marriage suffered from Beth's drinking issues, disagreements about whether to celebrate Hanukkah or Christmas, and in-laws that were constantly interfering in their life. But it was ultimately Beth's drinking and drug use that did the couple in.

Mike and Beth

"My friends and I were at this downright sleazy bar at a bachelor party when this gorgeous girl walked in with her friends. She definitely looked like she was too good for the place. I still remember working up the nerve to ask her to dance. I was 28 at the time and she was 24; we dated for five years before I proposed.

"Looking back, I think that I waited so long to propose because there were a lot of red warning flags flying high when we were dating. Her family was a big problem in a big way because they were all completely insane. Her crazy mother was constantly meddling in our life.

"Another flag that was waving that I ignored was Beth's drinking. I guess I thought of her as an extreme social drinker when we were dating. When she drank, she would get drunk, but not "happy" drunk. It would make her very bitter. I do remember asking her on our wedding day to please not drink a lot.

"At first things were fine. We had two kids. One of our major problems from the very beginning was that she had a very demanding and stressful job and worked a lot of hours. The other issue that caused many disagreements was religion. Beth is Jewish and I was born Christian, but I am not religious at all. I was fine with our kids being raised Jewish but I had always just assumed that we would have a Christmas tree at Christmas. That was not going to happen because my wife felt that her family would completely freak out if we had a tree.

"Apart from those bumps, we were pretty happy. We had two girls and we thought we would have one more to see if we would have a boy. I would have been happy with another girl, honestly, but I did think it would be nice to have a boy.

"We had what we thought was a perfectly healthy baby boy. When he was two months old, he went to sleep and just didn't wake up. The doctors were never sure if he had SIDS or another condition, but it didn't matter. It was absolutely devastating.

"The death of our son changed everything in our relationship. Beth was consumed by guilt and sadness and was always on edge. She would brood for days on end, and her drinking, which was already an issue, got worse. And she started to drink at all times of the day.

"We both should have gone to therapy, but we didn't. Because Beth's alcoholism made it impossible for her to reliably parent our two girls, I took over the majority of the parenting. It is very difficult to live with someone who is suffering and mourning and not dealing with it. I found out later, that Beth had started mixing prescription drugs with her drinking. I never knew what I would find when I came home. I once found her passed out at the top of our stairs. I probably should have figured it out because there were times that she would act drunk, but I couldn't smell any alcohol.

"Finally, Beth started going to a therapist, but it was not for the reason that I thought. She had met someone else on one of her frequent business trips and needed the therapist to help her find the courage, if you want to call it that, to leave me.

"When she left I was devastated. Not because I wanted to continue our marriage, which wasn't really a marriage anymore, but because it destroyed me to break up the family. I always had this picture of the happy mom, dad, and the kids."

Interesting Fact: Because many of the attorneys that I spoke to have been handling family law cases since the 1970's (and in some cases even earlier), they have witnessed various trends in addiction. Newport Beach, California attorney Steven Briggs said that in the seventies he witnessed a lot of marriages that were victims of alcoholism. In the eighties cocaine was a common marriage buster and in the nineties his clients were complaining that their spouse was addicted to a prescription drug. Lynn Gold-Bikin, a family law expert practicing in Norristown, Pennsylvania, says the she is now seeing a lot of marriages wrecked by addictions to the prescription drug Oxycontin. Whatever the addiction, the effect is the same. If left untreated, the addiction can ultimately destroy the marriage.

Is Alcohol or Drug Addiction Affecting Your Marriage?

The National Council on Alcoholism and Drug Dependence created a list of questions to help people determine if they have symptoms of alcoholism. (Many of these questions would apply to a drug addiction as well). Can you relate to these questions? Do they describe you or your spouse?

1) Do you occasionally drink heavily after a disappointment or a quarrel?
2) When you have trouble or feel pressure, do you drink more heavily than usual?
3) Can you handle more liquor than when you started drinking?
4) Did you ever wake up the morning after and discover you could not remember part of the evening before?
5) When drinking with others, do you try to have a few extra drinks when they will not know?
6) Do you feel uncomfortable at times if alcohol is not available?
7) Have you recently noticed that when you begin drinking, you are in more

of a hurry to get the first drink than you used to be?

8) Do you sometimes feel a little guilty about your drinking?

9) Are you irritated when family or friends discuss your drinking?

10) Have you noticed an increase in your memory blackouts?

11) Do you often wish to continue drinking after friends say they have had enough?

12) Do you usually have a reason for the occasion when you drink heavily?

13) When you are sober, do you often regret things you have done or said while drinking?

14) Have you tried switching brands or following different plans for controlling your drinking?

15) Have you often failed to keep promises to yourself about controlling your drinking?

16) Have you ever tried to control your drinking by changing jobs or moving to a new location?

17) Do you avoid family or close friends while you are drinking?

18) Are you having an increasing number of financial and work problems?

19) Do you sometimes have the shakes in the morning and find it helps to have a little drink?

20) Do you eat very little or irregularly when you are drinking?

21) Do you get frightened after you have been drinking heavily?

22) After periods of drinking, do you ever see or hear things that aren't there?

If you answered "yes" to several of the questions from 1 to 8, you may be in the early stage of alcoholism. Additional affirmative answers to several of the questions from 9 through 22 may indicate the middle to final stages of alcoholism.

Fix It

If alcohol and/or drugs are taking a toll on your marriage, here are some options.

- Talk to your family doctor about the situation. Most doctors can recommend a course of treatment that will work for your situation.
- Contact Alcoholics Anonymous (AA) at www.alcoholics-anonymous.org , (212) 870-3400 or Narcotics Anonymous (NA) at www.na.org or (818) 773-9999. (There are also groups that specialize in certain type of common addictions such as Cocaine Anonymous).
- Enter a treatment facility that has a reputation for success and has experience in treating your specific problem. Your doctor should be able to refer you to an excellent rehabilitation center.
- Check with your health insurance provider to see if your insurance covers treatment for addictions.
- In addition to pursuing the recommendations just mentioned, many people find it helpful to work with a therapist who has an expertise in helping people in your (or your spouse's) situation.
- A support group called Al-Anon has helped many spouses and children of alcoholics. They can be reached at: 1-888-4-AL-ANON (1-888-425-2666) and www.al-anon.alateen.org

Mental Illness and Divorce

"The incidence of depression is so great in America that it creates a lot of marital difficulties." James Feldman, Chicago, IL

Several studies put the incidence of depression in the United States at ten percent at any given time. Many family law attorneys told me that untreated depression is responsible for many divorces each year. Dallas family law attorney Mary McCurley told me that bipolar disorder (where a person appears at times manic and other times depressed) is also a common cause of divorce. Not surprisingly, mental illness also causes other symptoms of divorce like sexless marriages, and financial swings where someone's ability to make a living is affected. Ted and Susan's marriage was nearly decimated by Susan's depression.

Ted and Susan

"When I met Susan she was the poster child for someone with a positive attitude. She was absolutely the last person that you would expect to have depression. She did mention to me that she was depressed for a time in college, but nothing since. When I asked her about what her depression was like, she was very vague. It was clear that she didn't want to talk about it.

"When we married, she was thirty-two and I was thirty-four. She was very anxious to become a mother and we started to try to get pregnant right after our honeymoon. After a year of trying, nothing was happening and we started to get worried. Tests revealed that she had a fertility problem and we began special treatments right away.

"I had noticed a change in Susan even before we found out about the infertility. She was no longer the perpetually optimistic person that I married. She slept a lot, especially on weekends when she didn't have to get up for work. She stopped exercising, which was a big deal since she used to work out seven days a week. After she found out about the infertility, her mood just got worse. I did everything I could think of to reassure her that we would have a child even if that meant adopting, but she was still always down.

"I begged Susan to talk to a therapist, but she refused. I discussed her symptoms with her gynecologist who told us that it was not unusual for a woman who had a difficult time conceiving to experience depression. She suggested that we postpone the infertility treatments and that Susan take medication to help her with her problem. Meanwhile, Susan had taken a leave of absence from her job because she couldn't function well at work.

"Susan didn't want to take any medication because she wanted to pursue fertility treatments right away. There was no chance that she could have gotten pregnant accidentally at this time because our sex life was completely dead. Susan was not interested.

"I told Susan that I would not go ahead with the fertility treatments until she got help for her depression because I felt that even if she did get pregnant she couldn't parent a child. This caused a lot of fights between us and I was at the point where I just wanted to leave the marriage.

"Finally, I gave Susan an ultimatum. I told her that if she did not get help for her depression that I was going to leave her. I told her if she did get help, I would do everything that I could to support her, but that I was not going to stand by and watch her drown because she refused to grab hold of a life raft that was an inch from her hand.

"Thankfully, Susan grabbed onto the life raft. She called me at work and told me that she didn't want to lose me and was finally willing to get help. I called our doctor right away and got a name of a psychiatrist who specialized in treating depression.

"Susan's choice saved our marriage. She responded very well to medication, and continues to take it. She is a wonderful mother to our adopted daughter and everything is back on track including our sex life. But I know that if Susan didn't get help, everything would have gone the other way."

Do you or your spouse have symptoms of a mental illness? Fortunately, medical treatment is available. However, serious depression is not something that you can just talk yourself out of, or talk your spouse out of. It is not a question of just "cheering up." You or your spouse must discuss the problem with your family doctor who can direct you to the proper treatment.

I am including the symptoms of depression below because it was the mental illness that was most frequently cited by family law attorneys as a problem in some of the failed marriages that they see. If you feel that you or your spouse has any form of mental illness, I can't emphasize enough that you have to take immediate steps to get help.

The following questions concerning depression are from *WebMd the Magazine*. They recommend that if you answer, "yes" to these questions, and your symptoms (or your spouse's symptoms) have lasted more than two weeks, that you should consult a doctor.

- Do you have trouble doing or enjoying the things you used to do?
- Do you feel sad most of the time?
- Do you feel hopeless and/or worthless?
- Do you get tired for no reason?
- Do you sleep too little or too much?

Some of the other symptoms of depression are difficulty concentrating, stomach and digestive problems, decreased sex drive, recurrent headaches, weight loss or gain, thoughts of death or suicide. (From WebMD the Magazine/July/August 2005)

Fix It

Mental illness affects many marriages. If left untreated it can cause your marriage to come apart. If you suspect that you or your spouse is suffering from a mental illness, call your doctor today.

The Key Points

- Alcohol and drug addictions break up many marriages.
- When addicts seek help and follow a treatment program, their marriages are frequently salvageable.
- When the using spouse is in denial about the problem, the other spouse usually has no choice but to divorce so that the children aren't harmed, and to protect the family's assets.
- Mental illness is another frequent cause of divorce. Many forms of mental illness are treatable with medication.

SEVEN
DIVORCE SYMPTOM #7:
SPOUSE CLONES, STEPS, AND THE EX

"Although the divorce rate is high, I think that the more interesting statistic is the high percentage of divorced people who get remarried. People get remarried in high numbers because they recognize that the benefits of a good relationship are terrific."
Lawrence Stotter, San Francisco, CA

"Marriage is the triumph of imagination over intelligence, and second marriages are the triumph of hope over experience."
Dennis Wasser, Los Angeles, CA (quoting Oscar Wilde)

❖

Wouldn't you assume that the divorce rate for second marriages would be lower than the divorce rate for first marriages? Surely someone who had been dazzled by physical attraction the first time around would have learned that chemistry alone can't support a lifetime union. And those who entered first marriages with marital expectations shaped by romantic movies and novels surely have more realistic views of what a marriage is all about. It is perfectly reasonable to assume that most people learned from the mistakes that they made in their first marriages and wouldn't repeat those same mistakes in a second marriage. Certainly someone who was disappointed by his or her first marriage would do everything possible to ensure that divorce lightning does not strike twice.

All of these assumptions are wrong. Movie stars are not alone in finding out that second (third, fourth, and fifth) marriages usually fare worse than first marriages. Statistics show that second marriages are successful only about one-third of the time. Unlike first marriages that fail for many different reasons, most second marriages typically fail for one of two reasons. Reason one is that people fall victim to the clone syndrome and choose a second spouse that is very similar to their first spouse. The negative dynamic that ended the first marriage simply gets repeated with the new spouse. The second reason for the high rate of second marriage failure is that raising stepchildren, and dealing with former spouses, is so difficult that many second marriages collapse under the pressure.

Easy or not, second marriages are here to stay. More than seventy-five percent of people who get divorced eventually remarry. This accounts for the startling statistic that the percentage of weddings that are remarriages for at least one of the partners is forty-three percent.

The Clone Syndrome

"Second marriages fail for the same reasons as the first marriage. People marry the same jerk that they divorced both in terms of looks and personalities. I have represented clients through a third divorce where they married the same exact type of person for the third time." Joseph Gitlin, Woodstock, IL

"If you don't figure out what went wrong in your first marriage, the same thing will go wrong in your second marriage. That people marry the same kind of person again and repeat their mistakes is as powerful as the law of gravity." Allan Zerman, St. Louis, MO

Divorce lawyers from San Francisco to Miami told me that a major problem with second marriages is that the new spouse is often similar in personality, and usually looks, to the first spouse. I heard about a woman who married three alcoholics in a row, and a man who divorced one short, blond controlling woman to marry another short, blond controlling woman.

Southern California attorney John Schilling is not surprised when someone shows up in his waiting room for a second time with a future second wife who both looks and acts like the first wife. This is what he told me about the clone syndrome. "I have been around long enough that I am now representing divorced children of divorced parents, and have done divorces for some clients four or five times. People don't learn that they need to marry a different kind of person. They tend to marry the same person in terms of both looks and personality."

I wish I could cite some official study that proves the clone syndrome exists, but there isn't one. You will just have to take the word of family law attorneys who claim to see this pattern over and over again.

There is one important (occasional) exception to this rule. Where the person who went through a divorce has had significant post-divorce therapy to understand the role that he or she played in the marriage ending, the second spouse clone syndrome can be avoided.

Ken learned the hard way about the clone syndrome. It wasn't until his second marriage ended in divorce that he realized that he was a victim of the clone syndrome.

Ken and Andrea and Jane

"I married my first wife when I was twenty-four. She had this look about her that I had always been attracted to—she was very petite and was always put together. I think we dated for six months before I ever saw her without make-up. We often fought about how long it took her to get ready to go anywhere but I admit that she did look great when she finally got it together.

"Andrea was very ambitious. When we met, she was in law school and determined to graduate at the top of her class. She was obsessed with getting the right job at the right firm. I had my own business but I still had a lot of free time. My day was done at 5:00 p.m. and after that I would go to the gym and then meet Andrea for dinner. After dinner, she would go back to the library and study. We didn't spend as much time together as I would have liked but I always figured that when she was done with law school she would have a more normal life.

"We got married right after her law school graduation. She graduated with honors and I was thrilled for her. But the minute after we returned home from our honeymoon she started studying twenty-four/seven for the bar exam. During this time, I would hang out with friends because Andrea was never around. After her exam was over, she started to work at a law firm that really required a lot of hours. She would literally leave every morning at 7:30 and wouldn't get home before 8:30 or 9:00 p.m. When she was home, she usually just wanted to veg because she was wiped out from work. I was ready to go out because I had been sitting around waiting for her, but she was always too tired.

"Pretty soon all of our fights sounded the same. I would vent that I never saw her, and she would say that I didn't understand how much pressure she was under. This went on for about two years. Our sex life was becoming nonexistent. We were more like roommates than husband and wife.

"After a couple of years, she started coming home really late. She would tell me that she had a dinner meeting with an important client or had a seminar. Long story short, she had become involved with another lawyer in her office. That was marriage #1.

"Six months after we split up, I met Jane. To me she didn't look at all like Andrea. One was blond and the other brunette. But a lot of people thought that they did look alike, maybe because they both were short, petite, and attractive.

"Jane had just moved to Los Angeles from a small town in Wisconsin. She had always dreamed of becoming an actress, and moved to Hollywood to follow her dream. She took a lot of acting classes and went on a lot of auditions but she was always around at night, which is what I had missed when I was married to Andrea. We only knew each other eight weeks when I proposed. Looking back, that was too quick. But it felt right at the time.

"We got married in one of those little Las Vegas wedding chapels. My friends tried to warn me that I was getting remarried too soon, but I was stupid and didn't listen.

"I think in the back of my mind I thought that Jane would get discouraged, give up acting, and want to become a mom. But that is not what happened. She was tenacious in her quest to start a career. She started going to a lot of Hollywood parties to try to make connections. She always invited me to go along but that was really not my thing. On weekends, she would take extra acting classes and acting was all she ever talked about.

"After we were married for six months, I realized that I was in the same boat that I had been in with Andrea. I was married to another ambitious woman and I was spending my free time alone or with friends. Plus, Jane was in no hurry to have children, and wasn't one hundred percent sure that she wanted children. When it became clear our dreams were not reconcilable, we split up amicably. My second marriage only lasted one year."

I'm sure you can see what Ken initially missed. Although each of his wives had different career paths, both were extremely ambitious and directed. These type A women might have done fine with a type A man but Ken was one hundred percent type B.

After his second marriage ended, Ken said he took time off from dating, and spent some time in therapy to see where he had gone wrong. With the therapist's help, he realized that he had fallen victim to the clone syndrome.

Cure It

If you are currently divorced and plan to remarry some day, be aware of the clone syndrome. To avoid it, obtain therapy so that you understand why your marriage broke down and how your selection of your spouse played a part in it.

Stepchildren and Former Spouses

"When the stepchildren are not nice to their stepmother, but the father continues to

spend time and money on his children, the new wife resents it. All parties perceive it as who do you love more? Your kids or your new wife?" Herbert Palkovitz, Cleveland, OH

"Kids are great for a marriage, but stepchildren are anathema to a marriage." Norman Sheresky, New York, NY

Eleanor Brietel Alter, a longtime Manhattan divorce attorney, summed up the many problems that stepchildren create for second marriages this way. "Second marriages, where there are children still living in the home, are very difficult. Although it may be your house that the children are living in, you are not truly in control of the children. It is difficult to enforce rules in your house where the biological parent living in the other house has a different set of rules. Plus, it is hard for the new spouse not to resent that money is going out to the other household, or, the opposite, that the ex-spouse is not paying enough support. And, blending two sets of children can be very difficult. It is frequently difficult to feel the same about your kids and someone else's kids.

"I'll give you an example of what frequently occurs in stepfamilies. The new stepmom asks her stepchildren to make their beds. The kids respond that their mom doesn't make them make their beds at her house. The father of the children tells the new wife that he wants the kids to enjoy the time that they spend at their house so they shouldn't be required to make their bed. This type of dynamic is very common in stepfamilies."

Larry and Kim

Larry fell head over heels in love with Kim. Although it was her girl next-door look that first attracted him, it was their many common interests and values that sealed the deal. They met at a small, but fast growing software company that they both worked for. He knew from the photographs plastered all over her office that Kim had two elementary school age children at home. But the couple had barely returned from their honeymoon when the challenges of being a stepparent first appeared. This is how Larry remembered it:

"One of the first things that I admired about Kim was that she was a very devoted mother. We dated for a year before I actually met her two sons. She said that she wanted to make sure that we were the real deal before she brought me into their lives, which I really respected. But looking back, I can see how our dating life did not reflect the reality of married life with kids. When we were dating, Kim and her ex-husband shared custody. Her ex had the boys every other weekend, and two nights a week from school pick-up until bedtime. That was when Kim and I saw each other. We took romantic weekend trips out of town and went out for many nice dinners.

"When I finally met my future stepsons they were nine and eleven. I felt that we really hit it off but our time together was still fairly limited because Kim did not want me spending the night until we were married. Again, I agreed with her because I didn't want to set a bad example for the boys.

"The first couple of years things went fairly well. Kim and I had very different approaches to parenting and that came out fairly quickly. Kim doesn't like to set strict limits with the boys. She said that she prefers to be lax because their father is exceptionally strict but I always felt that was just an excuse that she used. I think the reason she was a weak parent was because she felt guilty both about the divorce and the fact that she worked a lot. She never said no to their constant requests for junk food and let them stay up until we went to bed.

"At first, I pretty much went along with Kim's approach in a somewhat transparent attempt to win over the kids. But other times I couldn't take it and would tell them that they needed to put away their toys or go to bed by 9:00. Kim never backed me up which left me feeling like the 'bad dad.'

"Kim told me before we got married that she did not think she wanted more kids, but agreed for my sake to have an open mind. After we were married a couple of years, I felt ready to have children and really wanted children of my own, but Kim felt that the baby years—the years of dirty diapers and sleepless nights—were finally behind her and she didn't want to start over again. We fought over this a lot.

"After a couple of years the boys transitioned from nice little boys to pre-teens who somehow learned all there was to know in life in just two short years. Now they just ignored my requests to pick up their things, and to do their homework. I would try to engage them in outdoor sports but they were pretty much glued to their video games and computers. We never truly bonded. They never said it but I always felt like they hoped that their parents would get back together and sort of saw me as the obstacle to that happening.

"In the midst of this stressful situation, the boys' father lost his job and got a court order which substantially reduced the amount of child support that he was required to pay. The child support money had been used for the kids' private school and now the pressure of making that payment fell to Kim and I.

"I really began resenting Kim for not wanting to have a child with me. I understood her reasons but I realized that I did not want to go through life without having a child of my own. Meanwhile, it seemed that whenever the four of us were together it was the three of them against me because Kim would never back me up.

"I started spending more and more time at work and on the golf course because I wanted to avoid Kim and the boys. Our marriage did not really end with a bang, more like a whimper. I moved out of the house on what would have been our fourth wedding anniversary."

I could fill an entire book with stories about second marriages that fell apart because of difficulties with step children, ex-spouses, and financial stresses caused by the pressure of supporting two households. I was told about a wife who left her second marriage because her stepson became involved in drinking and drugs, and uninvolved with school. Her concern for her own two children caused her to leave her second husband even though she still loved him. I was told about resentment by a second wife who felt like she had to work to make ends meet while her husband wrote substantial checks to his first wife for spousal and child support. And I was told about how tough it was to be stepparent. Not exactly a parent, but more than a friend, stepparents are not always able to navigate that great divide.

But if you are in a second marriage, you probably know all this. What you may not know is how to beat the odds and have a happy, successful second marriage that may not run as smoothly as The Brady Bunch, but runs nonetheless. Here are steps that you can take to make your second marriage last.

Fix It

Given how prevalent stepparenting is, it is surprising how few stepparents exist in popular culture. There is Cinderella's stepmother who undoubtedly deserves the "worst stepmother award." Julia Roberts' portrayal of a stepmother in the movie *Stepmom,* opened our eyes to how unappreciated stepparents are. (If Julia Roberts has a tough time, what hope is there for everyone else?)

The good news is that because stepparenting is so common today, there are many resources for stepparents that did not exist a generation ago. Some suggestions from these stepfamily experts appear below. But consider these suggestions to be just a start. Read some of the books on stepfamilies that I recommend below, get support from the Stepfamily Association of America, and if you still are having a difficult time with co-parenting stepchildren, consider marital or family therapy.

Stepparenting 101

- Do not make your spouse choose between you and his or her children.
- Do not badmouth your stepchild's parent in front of your stepchild.
- Beware of favoritism. Make sure that your family rules apply to all of the children living under your roof equally.
- Discuss and agree upon the role that you will play in your stepchild's life with your spouse. Sometimes stepparents take the role of a secondary

parent, other times they function better as an adult friend. If your stepchildren are teenagers, they can be included in the discussion.

- Do not get into arguments with your stepchild's biological mother or father; let your spouse handle difficult conversations with his or her ex. (Caveat: Sometimes stepparents are better able than their spouse to discuss things rationally with an ex-wife or ex-husband depending on the animosity that exists between the two former spouses. If this sounds like your situation, you might want to attempt dealing with the former spouse directly. However, make sure that you and your spouse are on the same page before you walk down that tightrope.)

Recommended Reading And Resources For Stepparents

Stepfamily Association of America
650 J Street, Suite 205, Lincoln, NE 68508
www.saafamilies.org
1-800-735-0329

Help! A Girl's Guide To Divorce and Stepfamilies
By Nancy Holyoke, American Girl, 1999

7 Steps to Bonding With Your Stepchild
By Suzen J. Ziegahn, Ph.d, St. Martin's Griffin, 2001

Stepcoupling: Creating and Sustaining a Strong Marriage in Todays Blended Family
By Susan Wisdom/Jennifer Green, Three Rivers Press 2002

Keys To Successful Step-fathering
By Carl E. Pickhardt, Barron's Educational Series, 1997

The Smart Step-Family
By Ron L. Deal, Bethany House Publishers, 2002

Second Wives: The Pitfalls and Rewards of Marrying Widowers and Divorced Men
By Susan Shapiro Barash, New Horizon Press, 2000
(For help in dealing with issues that are unique to a second marriage, whether or not stepchildren are involved).

Surprising Fact

Children don't stop wreaking havoc on second marriages simply because they leave the nest. Several divorce attorneys told me that they have handled many cases where adult children press elderly parents into divorces to protect their inheritances.

Seattle attorney Wolfgang Anderson explained: "When parents are in a second marriage and at an age where their adult children feel that they might die, kids frequently push for a divorce so that they can manipulate the estate. In fact, I have done three or four divorces of people in their eighties where the heirs pushed for the divorce. For instance, adult children from a second marriage might be concerned that adult children from a first marriage might inherit their parent's estate. These cases are not rare or unusual. I have had cases where one parent is in a nursing home, and the other is still in the house. The kids will say, 'Mom, you have to take care of us, or we are not going to have anything.'"

The Key Points

- Second marriages are challenging, but not impossible.
- Beware of the clone syndrome.
- Develop strong relationships with your stepchildren.
- Be civil towards your spouse's ex.
- Be understanding of your spouse's financial obligation to his or her children and former spouse.
- If your spouse is the non-custodial parent, encourage him or her to have a relationship with their children.

THE DIVORCE LAWYERS' GUIDE TO **STAYING MARRIED**

EIGHT
DIVORCE SYMPTOM #8:
GROWING APART

"If people grow together they will stay married. It doesn't matter which way they grow—to the left, right, up, down, or sideways—so long as they grow in the same direction. When the path of the two divides, and one goes one way and one goes the other way they are headed for a divorce."
Herndon Inge, Mobile, AL

❖

When a long marriage ends, one spouse usually explains the breakup with "we just grew apart." It is almost as if each spouse thought that they were using the same map, and didn't realize that their maps were different until they both showed up in different towns. A lot of bad things do "just happen" to people during the course of a lifetime, but growing apart from a spouse isn't one of those things. Couples grow apart because one or both spouses ignored growing apart symptoms until the growing apart was a fait accompli.

What are the symptoms of growing apart, one of the most common causes of divorce? I discussed that question with many of the family law attorneys that I interviewed. Their examples of how couples grow apart fit into eight scenarios: The Kidaholic, The Workaholic, The Hobbyholic, Age, Marriages Between Opposites, Changes in Goals and Values, Intellectual and Social Differences, and Marriages Between Straight and Gay Spouses. Each of these scenarios has its own symptoms. But you will also see that many of the scenarios and symptoms frequently overlap.

Two of these growing apart scenarios, age and opposites, are best prevented before the wedding. And, of course, where one spouse reveals (or is discovered) to be gay, the marriage is typically not salvageable. However, the other growing apart symptoms are absolutely curable if they are addressed before husband and wife venture too far off in different directions.

Scenario #1: The Kidaholic

"Children cause people to change their focus from caring about each other to caring about their children. Momma starts to put nearly all of her emphasis on her responsibilities toward her children, to the exclusion of her husband. There is no question that children are like leeches, and if you take your parental responsibilities seriously it is often difficult to find time for your spouse." Ellen Widen Kessler, New Orleans, LA

Did you ever notice that we have the term "workaholic" for someone who spends nearly every waking minute either at work, or thinking about work, but there is not a term for a parent, typically a mother, who spends every waking minute with her children, talking about her children, or doing something for her children? I call this woman a kidaholic.

Of course, men can be kidaholics, or both spouses can be kidaholics at the same time. I talk about woman here because the only time kidaholism negatively affects a marriage is when a husband feels like "he is somewhere at the bottom of the totem pole," at best, or off the pole completely, at the worst.

Today, thanks to the ubiquity of email, fax machines, laptops, and cell phones, a workaholic can get a work fix twenty-four/seven. The demands of motherhood are equally endless. Babies need us day and night for food, clean diapers, and cuddling. Daredevil toddlers need constant watching and attention. And there seems to be no end to the kid related errands that suck up most of a mother's day.

And just when mom thinks that she sees a light at the end of the nurturing tunnel with the ringing of the bell that denotes the start of kinder-garten, she becomes an afternoon slave to carpools, dance lessons, baseball, soccer, and basketball practice, homework, and school projects. Weekends are held hostage by playdates, kids' sporting events, and shuttling Joey Junior between birthday parties.

The problems that develop when a family's life is one hundred percent kid-directed and zero percent couple directed, is that when the kids grow up, the parents no longer have anything in common. Baxter Davis, an attorney practicing in Atlanta, described this frequent pattern.

"The husband is very busy making the money and the wife is very busy rearing the children, running the household, and spending the money. The wife is involved in maintaining the home and the vacation home, participating in the junior league and the PTA.

"When the kids turn fourteen or so, they begin to lose interest in their parents, and by sixteen kids can drive. Meanwhile, mom and dad have not developed common interests and common hobbies, because they were so busy doing their own things during the child rearing years. They simply didn't notice that they were drifting apart."

Miami attorney Cynthia Greene told me that a major complaint of many of her male clients is that they felt dumped by their wives after the kids were born. "Men are jealous of the time that their wife spends with the kids," Greene says. "Maybe jealousy isn't the proper word, because the men are being sincere, but where there is a total focus by the mother on the child, and no focus on the marriage or the husband, the marriage frequently falls apart. I have seen dozens of cases like this."

Santa Monica attorney Scott Weston pointed out that the difficult problem created for mothers is that "for a stay-at-home mom kids are a fulltime job; it is no different than a man being a workaholic. But where someone with a normal job can close the door to his or her office and go home, with kids the day never ends. The work doesn't manifest itself in cell phones and emails, it is very loving and doting; but it does take time away from the spouse. The mother needs to find a balance—time away from the kids and with her spouse."

I love the following letter, written to an advice columnist, for two reasons. First, it shows the pervasiveness of kidaholism and, second, and perhaps more importantly, it shows that most women have no idea how their husbands feel about the loss of attention.

"Dear [Columnist]: A fifth couple in our circle of friends recently ended their marriage. When I asked the husbands what happened, each said much the same thing: 'When we were first married, I was the most important person in my wife's life. With each child, my place was shifted farther and farther back until I felt totally forgotten.'

"These husbands told me that neglect made them vulnerable to someone who did show them some attention. You know the rest. When I asked the wives what happened, they said they didn't know—but guessed that they 'just drifted apart and their interests changed.' None of them knew how their husbands felt."

When you read Sara and Lee's story, notice that Lee used actions, not words, to "communicate" his hurt. This is very typical. Lee isn't going to win any awards for his communication skills, a "Honey, I'm feeling ignored...let's spend some time alone together" would undoubtedly have gone a long way. Still, he did express his displeasure in other ways. I'm glad that I could include their story in this book, because I think Lee's reaction is characteristic of how men behave when they feel ignored by their wife.

Lee and Sara

Like many people, Sara and Lee met at work. The two accountants worked hard all year, but from about the first of February through April 15th they practically lived at the office. They got to know each other well during late nights at the office during tax season.

In addition to their careers, they both had a lot in common. Both were avid athletes: they spent a lot of time biking and hiking together during their two-year courtship. They both loved good food and took turns cooking gourmet dinners for each other. Sara and Lee, both only children, each envisioned a large family.

"My wife became pregnant with our first child on our honeymoon or shortly after. I just remember that we were still writing thank you notes for our wedding gifts when we found out for sure that Sara was pregnant. We were both thrilled.

"We had discussed the stay-at-home versus working mom thing many times and Sara felt strongly that she wanted to stay home with the kids. Her mom had worked outside of the house from the time that Sara was little, and she still remembered how much she missed her mom being there when she came home from school. To make up for Sara's lost income, we decided that I would take on some additional consulting work, and that Sara would work part-time as soon as the children were in school.

"Our first child was a girl. We both fell in love with her immediately. I took off a week from work, and truly missed her when I returned.

"Our doctor and our friends warned us that the beginning would be rough but I don't think we were actually prepared for the reality of a baby. The baby woke up every two hours for the first three months. Sara was exhausted because she was breast-feeding exclusively and there wasn't much I could do besides change a diaper or two.

"The doctor had told us that we could have sex again six weeks after the baby's birth. Before we had kids, we had a great sex life. I didn't expect it to be exactly the same after kids but I still thought it would be pretty good. I counted down the six weeks, but Sally didn't seem to notice or care when the six-week sex moratorium was up. She said she was too exhausted for sex.

"Our routine changed drastically. Our morning workouts turned into pushing the baby in the stroller around the park. We did take-out instead of cook. When the baby was three months old, I suggested that we do a 'date night' without the baby. But Sara didn't feel comfortable leaving the baby with anyone, not even my mother. So the baby came with us on our dates.

"Sara became a completely different person when she became a mother. It was like none of her prior interests, including me, existed. I would go watch TV hoping that Sara would come and join me after the baby was asleep but she would work on the baby's scrapbook, or read one of those parenting books.

"It was four months before we had sex again. Sara couldn't believe that much time had passed but believe me, I had noticed! Things finally seemed to be getting a little bit back to normal. While most of Sara's time was devoted to the baby, she did go back to cooking on occasion and she bought one of those baby carriers so that we could start hiking again.

"When the baby was one, Sara got pregnant again. Unlike our first child, our second child needed to be held constantly. The instant you would put her down, she would cry. So the minute I got home from work, I would be responsible for watching one of the kids. We rarely went to bed at the same time and I started not to care. Sara was not into sex at all. I was always the initiator and she was rarely very into it.

"We really started to have separate lives. It is not like it happened on a specific day. We just fell into our own patterns over time. I kept in touch with some of my old friends and most of them did not have kids. Sara developed this whole new group of friends that she met at her mommy and me class. They pretty much would talk about some baby related issue. And when Sara and I talked, it was almost always about the kids.

"I would say that Sara probably thought that everything was pretty good between us but I really missed the conversations that we used to have about something that we were doing at work, or something to do with hiking or biking. Plus, our sex life had dwindled to something like once a month.

"I loved seeing the girls when I came home from work but Sara might as well have been a great nanny because she no longer had any real interest in being my wife. She didn't care at all about her appearance. She gained a lot of weight and didn't seem to care. She never dressed up anymore or put on make-up.

"I figured I would stick it out until the girls left for college but then I met someone at work who really took an interest in me. We started to spend a lot of time together as friends because she was also married. But one thing led to another, as they say, and we fell in love.

"I planned on keeping that relationship a secret, but Sara started being suspicious of all the time that I was spending on the computer after work. Basically, once the girls were asleep, I would start emailing my girlfriend. I was always careful about deleting the emails, but Sara somehow pulled one up when I was at work and went ballistic.

"There was no way she was forgiving me, and she didn't think that the affair was in any way her fault. We went to therapy a couple of times but she felt like I should have told her that I felt left out instead of having an affair. I felt like it should have been obvious to her that we were living in the same house but had grown apart. We pretty much spent the hour in therapy pointing fingers at each other, so we stopped going and called the marriage quits."

Does this sound like your life?
Are you a kidaholic or are you married to one?
Kidaholic Symptoms
- Kidaholics tend to talk primarily about their children.
- Nearly all of a kidaholic's interests or activities outside the home somehow relate to their children (scrapbooking, soccer mom, school volunteer).
- Kidaholics frequently give up interests that they had before they had children.
- Kidaholics frequently part ways with old friends who do not have children.
- Kidaholics frequently will not go away with just their spouse for even one night even where there is another capable adult to care for the child.
- Spouses of kidaholics complain that "there is no time for me."
- Spouses of kidaholics complain that their sex life is lacking.
- Kidaholics generally do not make time to spend alone with their spouse.

Cure it

The irony of being a kidaholic is that in trying to be a perfect mother, the marriage suffers. And, as you already know if you have gotten to this point in the book, one of the best things that you can do for your children is raise them with the role model of a happy, successful marriage. The other good news is that being a good parent and being a good spouse are not mutually exclusive.

If you suspect that your spouse feels like they are neglected, or that since you became a parent the only thing that you and your spouse have in common is the children, consider making the following changes:

Keep a regular weekly date night with your spouse. (Of course, common sense applies here. If your baby is an infant and still nursing, your baby gets to come to the date and snooze in her car seat.)

Spend a weekend alone with your spouse at least a couple of times a year.

Don't forget about your sex life. Many women feel "touched out" after spending the day with a couple of clinging toddlers. Remember that your spouse has not received the same amount of touching (hopefully) during the day.

Figure out a hobby that you and your spouse can do together as a couple on a regular basis. It can be anything from jogging together in the morning to watching old movies on DVDs together at night.

Scenario #2: The Workaholic

"The consequence of workaholism is emotional neglect of the marriage. The pattern goes like this. The workaholic doesn't pay attention to his or her spouse. The spouse becomes jealous of the workaholic's exciting outside life. That spouse becomes argumentative and the workaholic gets annoyed with the constant complaining." Hanley Gurwin, Bloomfield Hills, MI

I interviewed a man named Jack who freely admitted to being a workaholic during a good portion of his marriage. At the end of my interview with Jack two things struck me. First, the cause of his divorce would be difficult to characterize because his marriage had been plagued by many different symptoms of divorce. During his ten-year marriage, Jack and his wife Janice experienced huge financial swings, infidelity, and a dwindling sex life. Although his marriage was challenged by many divorce symptoms, I think the single biggest factor in the dissolution of Jack's marriage was the affair that he was having with his dynamic career, and that is why his story is profiled in this chapter.

The second thing that struck me about Jack was that he seemed to have spent a lot of time analyzing his failed marriage and the large role that he had in its demise. Typically, there is a lot of finger pointing at the other spouse. When Jack pointed fingers he pointed them at himself. In fact, he could not say enough nice things about his ex-wife who he hoped would take him back one day. Here is the story of Jack's marriage to Janice.

Jack and Janice

When Jack and Janice met in 1989 they both were just nineteen years old. Janice, an aspiring actress, worked as a cocktail waitress while waiting for her big break. Jack, a college student, waited tables at the same bar to help offset his educational expenses. Although Jack and Janice are both exceptionally attractive, it was not love at first site. Jack mistakenly assumed that someone as beautiful as Janice would be shallow and conceited. Janice's first impression of Jack—that he was a handsome, cocky guy with a one-track mind—were also off base. In time a friendship developed and then a romantic relationship. Next, came a key to Jack's apartment followed by a furniture mover. They married in 1994, five years after their first meeting.

Both Jack and Janice were extremely ambitious. Janice had found an agent, and had landed a few national television commercials. Jack started a computer software company in the late 1990s and things were going unbelievably well. He admitted to me that he worked round the clock. His goal was to get the company to a place where it could be taken public. He fantasized about being the "next Bill Gates." The money was phenomenal.

Meanwhile, he urged Janice to give up her career ambitions because he was concerned that an acting career "would require her to be gone all the time." Jack felt that Janice should stay home with their two young boys and he wanted her to be home on those rare occasions that he was home.

Jack confessed that the success of his business had gone to his head. "It made me feel powerful and beautiful women were throwing themselves at me. Meanwhile, my wife never seemed interested in having sex with me. I know now that it was because she was upset at me for putting the brakes on her career ambitions while I was going full steam ahead with mine. In contrast to my wife, these other women were continually feeding my large ego by telling me how hot I was." Jack admitted that he had many brief relationships with the numerous women who were experts at feeding his self-esteem.

The crash of the dot.com industry in the late nineties decimated Jack's financial dreams.

"I can't tell you how devastated I was by the failure of my business. But it did wake me up to the fact that I had a wife and two kids at home that were the most important things in my life. Without my work to consume me, I had this epiphany that I was completely in love with my wife."

But for Janice, who had spent the last several years married to a workaholic, Jack's confessions of love were too little, too late. She had become detached and resentful of Jack because he had asked her to give up her career, but he hadn't been willing to cut back at all on his career for her or their two boys. Plus, she suspected his extramarital affairs.

Jack felt that if he wanted his marriage to continue, he needed to be completely honest. "I came clean with Janice about my affairs and we went to counseling. At first, Janice maintained that she was willing to try to get through this test in our marriage, but that it would take time. She said she still loved me, but she really never invested herself into counseling the way that I did. It was like Janice was so used to not having me in her life because I was an absent husband for so many years that she didn't know how to fit me back in. Plus, our sex life continued to be absolutely terrible."

"Janice decided she didn't want to continue with the counseling or with me. She never got over resenting me for cherishing my career more than I cherished her and her career, and for being an emotionally and physically absent father.

"I lead a much more balanced life now. I still work hard but I don't let it consume me the way that it used to. Janice and I have a very friendly relationship because of the kids. I date, but I won't get seriously involved with anyone else because I want to be available in case Janice ever gets to the point where she would consider taking me back."

Symptoms of workaholism

There is a fine line between being a worker with a demanding job, and a workaholic. There are many careers that simply require a lot of hours. Consider these symptoms of a true workaholic.

- Workaholics have very few interests not related to work.
- Workaholics refuse to (but could) take time off from work for important events like a child's graduation or a close friend's wedding.
- When a workaholic attends a non-work function their head is still at work.
- Workaholics "work" when they are not at work. They make "work calls" during family dinners and read email on their wireless phone during your Saturday night dinner date.
- Spouses of workaholics frequently complain that "you put work before me."
- Some workaholics don't ever develop close relationships with their children because they are rarely home.

Cure It

Some workaholics are like Jack and ultimately experience a major life event—a health scare, a business failure, or the death of a close friend or relative—that helps them get their workaholism in check. However, for many workaholics, therapy is the only thing that can temper their addiction to work.

Scenario #3: The Hobby Addict

"It is okay if spouses have divergent interests—for example, he likes baseball, she likes to knit—but to make a marriage last they must have similar interests as well." Hanley Gurwin, Bloomfield Hills, MI

I came across a great cartoon the other day that exemplified marriage to a hobby addict. Two female guests at a wedding are inspecting the couple's wedding cake. Sitting on top of the cake is the traditional plastic bride in a veil holding a bouquet of flowers. Next to her is a plastic groom sitting on a couch, facing a large screen TV and gripping an outstretched remote. Needless to say, the groom's attention is fixated on the television, not on his bride. One of the guests comments, "Well, at least she seems to know what she's getting into."

The husband in the cartoon came to his marriage with his "hobby" already in existence. But a spouse can become excessively involved with a new pastime any time during the marriage. In fact, empty nests and retirement are common times for people to pour themselves into a hobby that they had just dabbled in when work or kids were taking up most of their time. Lawyers told me about clients who felt abandoned by retired spouses who got caught up in the bridge circuit, began training for marathons, or would not get off the golf course.

Any diversion that takes one spouse away from the marriage frequently, and leaves the other spouse feeling deserted can cause problems in a marriage. Hobby obsessions that are exclusive to one spouse will have the same effect on a marriage as workaholism or kidaholism. The couple will grow apart.

An attorney practicing in Irvine, California swore to me that the following story is true. The attorney's client, an elderly man, wanted a divorce after

47 years of marriage. According to the man, his wife was having an affair with his longtime golf partner. But the man said he didn't want the divorce because he was angry about the infidelity. Rather, the man was angry because the affair caused his golf partner to have a nearly fatal heart attack while he was making love with his "friend's" wife. He wanted a divorce because he was angry at his wife for nearly killing his golf partner.

Are you or your spouse obsessed with a hobby or activity that does not involve your spouse?

Symptoms of a Hobby Addict

- One spouse frequently complains that the other spouse's hobby is taking up all of his or her time.
- The hobby addict doesn't devote a significant amount of time to the marriage.
- The hobby is so time consuming that the spouse has no time for other interests that could include his or her spouse.
- One spouse frequently complains that he or she feels like a "baseball, golf, bridge, exercise, etc." widow.

Cure It

If you feel like your spouse's hobby is causing the two of you to grow apart, discuss the following alternatives with your spouse.

- Are there ways for you to become involved in the hobby? Even if you can't participate or don't want to participate, find out about the hobby so that you can discuss the hobby with your spouse.
- Carve out "couple time" with your spouse each week where you do som thing together that you both enjoy.
- Talk to your spouse about adding a regular activity to your life that you both enjoy.
- If your spouse is unreceptive to your suggestions, make an appointment with a good marriage counselor who had help you find a compromise.

Scenario #4: Age at Time of Marriage

"The age at which one marries is significant. Young marriage doesn't work today. People should wait until they are in their early thirties and have had some life experience."
Lowell Sucherman, San Francisco, CA

"People who marry in their twenties are subject to discovering that they have diverging goals for life or marriage. The time between twenty-three and thirty is major growth time-that is why we have the seven year itch." Tony Dick, Sacramento, CA

It is not a coincidence that Oklahoma has the second highest divorce rate of any state (1990 statistics show 7.9 divorces per 1,000 compared to Massachusetts with 2.7 divorces per 1,000). Oklahoma also has one of the lowest average ages for first marriages: 22 for women and 24 for men, compared to the national median age for first marriages which is 26.9 for males, and 25.3 for females. And think about this: The National Marriage Project (Rutgers University) has cited studies that demonstrate that teenage marriages are two to three times more likely to end in divorce compared to marriages at an older age.

I interviewed 100 attorneys and not a single one recommended getting married at a young age. Not one. When it came to giving marital advice, many divorce attorneys warned against getting married before the age of twenty-five, and several others suggested that people wait until they are at least thirty before tying the knot. Jackie's story would have fit well in many places in this book. I think that it fits best into this chapter because her age and inexperience caused her to misinterpret the many red flags that her spouse was flying.

Jackie and Andrew

Jackie wasn't an official model at age 21, but she looked like one. Andrew, a 35-year-old affluent entrepreneur noticed her immediately when she came to work at his company. Jackie defied the dumb blond stereotype. She graduated high school with honors, and finished college in just three years. But her high IQ did not protect her from being swept off her feet by the gregarious and successful Andrew. They married less than a year after they met. This is what Jackie said about her troubled marriage:

"Marrying at twenty-two was a big mistake. It seems trite, but I was no doubt looking for daddy. I had had many issues with my own father. He was a brilliant, well-respected scientist who had published many groundbreaking articles in his field and was frequently quoted in the media. But my father was an observer of the world and consequently not very emotional.

"With Andrew, I mistook his outgoing nature and financial generosity with an ability to connect emotionally. In hindsight, I now see that, like my father who appears very interesting to the outside world but is not at all nurturing, Andrew was not emotionally available as a husband. Andrew was very much like my dad. On the surface they are both engaging, but neither could truly connect on a deep emotional level with people.

"Immediately after we were married, I sublimated my personal hopes and desires. Andrew traveled a lot and he wanted me to be with him so I quit my job.

"Two years after we married we had a son. Being a mother caused me to grow up quickly. I went from being an adoring trophy wife who liked being taken care of to being a mother and having a very different sensibility. I basically changed from a girl to a woman. Of course, if I had waited to get married, I would already have been a woman and the change would not have been as dramatic.

"But the change in me was major. It was like the world had tilted on its axis. And all of a sudden I saw Andrew for who he really was. Where I once thought he was a person of conviction, I now saw him as rigid. He drank a lot when we were dating and at the time I thought that meant he was fun-loving. Once I had grown up, I realized that his drinking was extreme and constant like an alcoholic. He would drink coffee and caffeinated soda all day and when his hectic day was over, he would polish off a bottle of wine by himself each night. On those rare days when he wasn't working he would start drinking wine as early as 10:00 a.m.

"After we were married a couple of years, Andrew began to have career troubles and ultimately financial troubles. This only made Andrew drink more. He continued to blame others for his problems. He controlled our money completely. He was in complete denial when it came to our new financial situation and he went through all of our savings as well as our son's college fund.

"I left after seven years. Although Andrew's drinking provided me with a good excuse to get out of the marriage, the truth was that I married a person who felt right at twenty-two but was wrong when I grew up.

"If I had gotten married when I was older, a lot of this would have been avoided. Andrew made me get rid of my college pictures because he didn't want to see me with other guys. Clearly, he was very jealous. When I was young, jealously felt like love to me. Now that I am older, I see it as controlling.

"I'm completely not the person that I was then."

Interesting Fact: Age at the time of marriage really has two aspects. One, of course, is that people who marry at too young of an age frequently find themselves divorced. Another aspect of the relationship between age and marriage that is frequently overlooked is a large difference in ages between the spouses. Typically this arises where the marriage is a second (or third) for one of the spouses.

Lowell Sucherman, an attorney who handles high-end divorce cases in San Francisco, commented that large age differences cause problems because people end up in different places down the road. When one party is getting ready to retire, the other one is just getting started in their career. When one party is slowing down due to advancing age, the other party still feels young and wants to be active.

Symptoms

- You feel like you and your spouse are growing apart because you married at a young age and your partner no longer fits you, or
- There is a large age difference between you and your spouse and you feel like you are at different places in your life.

Cure It

If you have children together, it is important that you and your spouse see a marriage counselor to reconcile the problems caused by marrying at an early age. Remember, if you have children together, a divorce will get your spouse out of your house but not out of your life.

Scenario #5: Elephants Don't Marry Giraffes

"The movie "The Odd Couple" is a good example of why opposites don't make for a good marriage." Donn Fullenweider, Houston, TX

Donn Fullenweider, a family law attorney with a practice based in Houston, Texas, has seen many marriages crumble due to the opposite natures of the parties. He told me about a woman client that he had; a right brained, creative thinker, who was married to a linear thinking engineer. His female client summed up how differently they viewed the world: "If my husband made a paper airplane and sailed it though the air, he would be interested in the physical factors that caused the airplane to fly while I saw just a beautiful freeform figure." The woman's soon to be ex-husband was a detail oriented, rule follower, and she was just the opposite. The things that were important to her were not important to him, and vice versa.

We have all heard the old saying that "opposites attract." The may attract, but they don't seem stick. In fact, while many divorce attorneys mentioned that it is fine and healthy to have different interests, spouses need to be more alike than different to make it to a silver wedding anniversary. Manhattan attorney Norman Sheresky told me that he heard a family law judge, who saw thousands of marriages fail when an Oscar Madison married a Felix

Unger, sum up the problem when he said, "Elephants don't marry giraffes."

Jennifer was an elephant who married a giraffe, or maybe it would be more accurate to say that she was a bulldog who married a sloth. Fortunately, Jennifer ended things before she and her husband Max had children.

Jennifer and Max

It was hard not to like Jennifer. Her smile was wide, and her voice was energetic. She did not have to tell me she was driven. We met in her office at a mid-sized talent agency where she had recently landed her dream job as a music agent. Although her phone kept ringing and her computer constantly clicked as emails arrived, she kept her promise to ignore both for the duration of our interview. On her office coffee table was a magazine whose cover featured a picture of a woman squeezed into a funky vintage dress. When I commented on it, she mentioned that she had designed the size four dress that strained against the cover model's size 10 body. Clearly, Jennifer was an ambitious woman. Yet, it was her passion for work and new experiences that ultimately caused her to leave her husband.

"When my husband and I started dating, he was thirty-one and I was twenty-six years old. After two years of dating, we lived together for one year, and then we got married. When I met Max, I thought I was ready to settle down with someone 'nice.' But we were not married long when Max's lack of drive began to bother me. I am very driven and Max is a great guy but he is very content with the status quo. He works nine-to-five at a job that he neither loves nor hates, and seems perfectly fine with that. Our ambitions are completely different. It has nothing to do with money. It has everything to do with having a passion for life and everything life offers. Ultimately, Max's lack of drive made me crazy. I couldn't relate to his lack of ambition and he never understood what made me tick.

"After we were married for a couple of years, Max was ready to move on to the next stage and have kids. The thought of having children terrified me because I knew that if we had kids together I would stay with him for the sake of the kids. I was very, very concerned that in the long run we would simply have nothing to talk about. He did not stimulate me at all mentally. I think that is why I fell out of love with him. We are very, very, different people.

"Therapy helped me realize that I had been living a life that was my mother's life; a predictable suburban life. But it was not the life that I wanted. Once I realized that, I also realized that it would be wrong to continue with the marriage. Max and I both deserved to be with people who appreciated us for who we were."

Newport Beach, California lawyer Jacqueline Whisnant described how these elephant/giraffe marriages disintegrate: "When one person is a linear thinker—a planner-saver type, and the other person is a more creative person, they have different approaches to life and end up losing respect for the other person." Jennifer and Max's marriage is a good example of what Whisnant described. Ultimately, Jennifer lost respect for Max's life outlook.

Shari and Matt

Although Shari's story includes infidelity, she ultimately realized that the demise of her marriage had more to do with her husband's search for some-one who shared his disposition (he was looking for another giraffe), and less to do with the adventure of a sexual affair.

"Matt and I met in college, and got married when we were just twenty-one. We dated for less than a year before we got married, which was not long enough. Our romance was a whirlwind. He was charming, smart, and great looking. But almost immediately after the wedding, I was already wondering, 'Who is this guy?' We bought a house and had a baby and soon eleven years had passed. When I was pregnant with our second child, I discovered that he had been having an affair with his secretary. He then spent several months doing a slash and burn on my emotions.

"I knew that the relationship was completely over when he came to the hospital for the birth of our second daughter, and his first words to me were

'This is the worst day I have ever had in my life.' He went on to marry his secretary and they had two children together.

"My ex changed a lot when he married this other woman, or maybe he just went back to who he really was. I am a very creative, free spirit type. Most of my friends are artists, my family is very entrepreneurial, outdoorsy, and strong democrats. My ex is very conservative. His family had always pressured him to be financially successful and his second wife did as well. He married a woman who was a lot like his mom in terms of personality type and values. Maybe she was a better match for him. Our two girls can't believe we were ever together because we are so opposite."

Symptoms of a marriage of opposites
- You have lost respect for your spouse because your personalities or outlooks are completely opposite.
- You feel like your spouse doesn't understand you because you are so different.

Cure It
People who are opposites usually had something that brought them together in the first place. Find an excellent therapist to help you work through your issues.

Scenario #6: Different Goals and Values
"Marriages frequently end because one spouse changes the rules deep into the marriage. It can be the woman wanting to go back to work after the kids are out of the house, or some other significant change in the family pattern." Marshall Wolf, Cleveland, Ohio

There are two aspects to this all too common cause of divorce. Some people have different goals and values from the date of their first wedding anniversary. I talked about this significant issue in Chapter Two: Unrealistic Expectations.

But even where a couple had similar goals and values on their wedding day, that doesn't mean that one or both spouses won't develop different goals and values over the course of the marriage that conflict with the expectations and desires of the other spouse. To make things even more complicated, sometimes a couple appears to have the same ultimate goal, but has very different ideas on how to achieve that goal. Sacramento divorce attorney Anthony Dick told me that sometimes the marital problem is related to differences in methodology: "Both parties can have the same goal of going to New York, but if one spouse wants to walk there and the other spouse wants to get there sitting in United Airline's first class section, there will be problems."

When one spouse has a goal that can't be reconciled with a long-standing marital routine, the couple frequently parts company. Ron and Lynn's marriage nearly followed this pattern. It was only because of a major compromise on Lynn's part that the marriage ultimately survived.

Ron and Lynn

"I have always been a big city girl, and still consider myself one even though I no longer live in a big city. I love to shop and go out to lunch with girlfriends. The noise and traffic really never bothered me like it bothers some people. Ron and I had been work friends for years before we 'discovered' each other.

"In fact, I had complained to Ron for years about a commitment-phobic boyfriend that I had when I was in my mid-30s. We finally broke up after I had wasted five years waiting for him to propose. I was kind of like that popular cartoon where the woman hits herself in the head and says something like, 'Oh my God, I forgot to have children!'

"Fortunately, Ron who was 40 and single (he had a short marriage right after college) did not have the same commitment problem. We got married about a year after we started dating. Everything was great except that when I tried to get pregnant, I couldn't. Ron and I talked a lot about it and decided that we would be a wonderful aunt and uncle to our many nieces and nephews, but that we wouldn't have kids of our own.

"For years, we had a very happy life living on the upper west side of Manhattan. But where I loved the hustle and bustle of the city, Ron was the happiest when we went to the country for summer weekends. For vacations, he wanted to go somewhere in the mountains where life was slow. I preferred to vacation in big cities.

"One time we rented this great cabin kind of house by a gorgeous lake in the Northwest. Ron just sort of announced that he was fed up with living in New York and wanted to move to a smaller town. There really wasn't much of an issue as far as his work was concerned because he did most of his work out of a home office. I told him that I absolutely couldn't leave the city.

"I remember that the rest of that trip was pretty well shot. It was like I had knocked the life out of him. I think he had harbored the dream of moving out of the city for a long time but was afraid to bring it up.

"Months went by and we didn't talk about what Ron said again. But I could tell that he was unhappy. His entire disposition had changed and we started to argue about the most ridiculous things. I'm not sure if Ron would have ultimately left me for the country or not, but I also saw that I wasn't being fair by forcing him to stick to what had become our status quo.

"I finally told him that I was open to a compromise. If he could find a country area that he loved that was within a two-hour drive to a big city, I would be willing to move. That was all it took. Before I knew it, our apartment was listed in the real estate section and we had put a down payment on a home that was on two acres of land just northeast of Santa Barbara, California. It really was a good compromise, because Santa Barbara was just about an hour away and had movie theatres and restaurants, and Los Angeles was just over a two-hour drive.

"I am surprised that the move worked out as well as it did. I still get back to New York a lot to see family and friends but I don't miss it the way that I thought I would. I have a great job where I live now and Ron is very,

very happy and grateful that I was flexible enough to try something new."

Symptoms of a change in values and goals

- One spouse wants to make a major life change that substantially changes the marital status quo.
- Common examples of changes include a woman wanting to start a career after the children are in school or out of the house, the breadwinner wanting to change careers, someone becoming more or less interested in a common religion or wanting to change religions, one spouse wanting to move, and retirement.

Cure It

If your spouse wants to make a major life change and it is one that you can support, you should. Marriages are not static and people are not static. The marriages that make it are the ones that support and encourage positive change in the other spouse. If you feel strongly that the proposed change would be detrimental to your relationship, then you and your spouse must consult an experienced marriage counselor to work through the issue.

Scenario #7: A Gap In Success

"Many long-term marriages break up because someone has changed in a significant way and they no longer work as a couple." Rita Bank, Washington, D.C.

I'm not sure if you can call it a trend exactly, but many attorneys commented that they have a new type of client appearing more frequently in their offices over the last few years — extremely successful women who claim to have outgrown their husband. Of course, the only thing that is truly new is that the person doing the complaining is a woman. For years, divorce attorneys have watched as successful men in long term marriages shed wives that no longer fit the bill.

Cleveland attorney Marshall Wolf explained the pattern this way: "Sometimes one spouse grows professionally and the other one doesn't.

Where they were a compatible couple early on in their marriage, now they are not. "The 'left behind' spouse blames it on someone else, but typically the left behind spouse has not kept up physically (appearance), emotionally, and/or intellectually with the other spouse."

Another related phenomenon that occurs when one spouse becomes very successful during the marriage is what I call the "Adulation Factor." The successful spouse receives a tremendous amount of respect and adulation in the work place but the other spouse treats him or her just like, well, a normal spouse. Boston attorney David Lee explained the problem this way: "When one party receives lots of positive recognition at work and then goes home and is asked to take out the garbage, the successful person hears a negative. That, combined with not receiving praise for his great success when he is at home, causes divorces."

Salt Lake City attorney David Dolowitz told me a story about one of his clients that exemplified the problem that frequently develops when there is a wide success gap between spouses. "I had a case where my client did everything exactly as her husband wanted and ended up divorced because what her husband ultimately wanted was a spouse who was nothing like the wife that he had created. My client told me that she and her husband had met in high school and got married after graduation because that is what her husband wanted. He also wanted her to stay home and raise the kids and work with the Mormon relief society, so she did. Ultimately, her husband left his stay-at-home wife for another woman that he had met through business." Throughout the divorce proceeding, Dolowitz's distraught client, who had followed all of her husband's rules, kept insisting, "He can't divorce me."

Nancy is one of those new successful female clients that divorce lawyers are increasingly seeing. She was very matter of fact about how she simply outgrew her husband.

Nancy and Tony

"I met Tony in law school. Looking back, there were signs all over the place about the differences in our drive. I strived to be on law review and graduate with honors. Tony only cared that he graduated. That same pattern prevailed after law school.

"Because I had very good grades and graduated near the top of my class, I pretty much had my choice of jobs. I went to work at a large Chicago firm and, from day one, strived to make partner. I joined the right bar associations and began to specialize in tax work. Our clients were mostly Fortune 500 type of companies. Right away I worked on client development. Several nights a week I would take clients or potential clients out for dinner.

"Tony was just not as motivated, which didn't really bother me at first. I worked long hours and it was nice knowing that he would be there when I got home. He had a normal nine to six existence at a small firm that did employment law which meant that he had time to take care of a lot of the household things that I didn't have time for.

"Three years out of law school, I was making twice as much as Tony. This didn't seem to bother him but it did bother me. Before I knew it, ten years had passed. We basically spent Saturday nights together and had breakfast on Sunday mornings. But that was about it. We had completely separate social groups. I don't mean to sound like a snob but the people in my world were extremely bright and interesting business people.

We truly just grew apart. We no longer had similar friends, my tastes had changed, and our professional goals were very different.

"We had been married for ten years and Tony wanted to start a family but said he didn't want his kids to have a mom that they never saw. And I really wasn't willing to slow down. I wasn't even sure that I wanted kids.

"Our marriage ultimately just fizzled out. My feelings for Tony were gone, and so was everything that we once had in common."

Symptom

- One spouse, usually due to their chosen career, begins to cultivate a vastly different intellectual and social circle than the other spouse.

Cure It

This is one of those symptoms where just being aware of it is half the battle. If you feel like your marriage is traveling down this road, or could travel down it some time in the future, you and your spouse need to develop a plan so that both of you end up in a similar intellectual and social place.

Scenario #8: Marriages Between Straight and Gay Spouses

"I am seeing an increase in divorces as a result of a spouse's changing sexual preference. And, I see it with both gay men and lesbians." Mabry De Buys, Seattle, WA

It seems like about once a month, an advice columnist will print a letter from either a married homosexual man who is struggling with a secret life, or a woman married to a gay man who is at a loss on how to proceed. This letter is typical:

"Dear [Columnist]: I am a 38-year-old married gay man. I am having a very difficult time dealing with this issue. My wife and I are divorcing. The truth came out when I went into rehab after becoming addicted to prescription pain medication. I realize I have made a mess of everything. I love my wife of 15 years but I am unable to love her the way she deserves."

Nearly all of the attorneys that I spoke to had handled divorce cases that resulted from either a husband or wife having a preference for the same sex. According to Carol Sever in her book *My Husband is Gay*, two percent of all married men are basically homosexual, and one in five gay men, or twenty percent, are married or have been married in the past.

Why would someone gay marry someone who is straight? In some cases there is denial or a lack of awareness of the sexual preference. Other times, gays marry straights because of a desire to conform to social or religious expectations. Sometimes it is simply because of a desire to raise children in a traditional family. Sandra's husband Harvey married because he wanted a "normal" life in the heterosexual world.

Sandra and Harvey

If you were gay in the nineteen fifties, sixties, or the early seventies you could forget about coming out of the closet. Most of America didn't even acknowledge that there was a closet let alone one with a door. Gay pride festivals weren't featured on TV, gays fought in the military but we pretended that they didn't, and gay marriage described a heterosexual couple that was very happy. To be openly gay meant limited job opportunities and never fathering a child. But a sexual preference is not an easy thing to hide and consequently many marriages between heterosexuals and closeted gays ultimately failed.

Sandra told me about her marriage to a gay man. Sandra and her husband married in 1960 and the marriage ended traumatically seven years and two children later. Here is her story.

"When I was a senior in high school, a close friend asked if he could give my telephone number to Harvey. I was okay with it because Harvey was good-looking, personable, and the rare twenty-year-old with a car in New York City. I was wined and dined and we were married three years later. It was a very happy time in my life.

"Harvey was in sales and very good at what he did. He was a wonderful provider, and was always bringing me back lovely gifts from his frequent business trips. Before long we moved from New York City to Phoenix, Arizona where we started a family. I remember consciously thinking how lucky I was to have a husband who loved me, a gorgeous baby boy, and a beautiful home.

"Time passed and soon I was the mother of two boys. But something had changed in my marriage. I couldn't put my finger on it then and I can't even put my finger on it now, but something had changed between us. The best way that I can explain it is that Harvey had become distant and we had frequent arguments. I just knew in my gut that there was something that wasn't right. Even though marriage counseling wasn't common at that time, I insisted that we visit a therapist.

"The counselor wanted to see us separately at first. At one of my appointments, the counselor asked me several highly personal questions concerning sex, including whether or not I had ever had oral sex. In those days, most of us waited until we were married before we had sex, and Harvey was the only man that I had ever been intimate with. I found the questions strange and asked the therapist if he had asked Harvey the same questions. The therapist said he had but insisted that if I wanted to know how Harvey responded that I would have to ask him.

"When Harvey came home from work that evening I confronted him. I said, 'What did you say in response to the sexual questions that the therapist asked?' At first Harvey did not want to answer me but I pushed him, and he finally did. He admitted to sexual practices that we had never done together. I started screaming, 'With who! Tell me with who!' He finally mentioned the names of two men who he worked with and who had been over to our home several times for dinner. I still remember my reaction. The room started spinning and the floor felt like it was dropping out from under me. It was a horrible, horrible nightmare, but this is how I found out that my husband was gay.

"Harvey had been having affairs with men throughout our marriage. He knew that he was gay when he married me because he had homosexual relationships that predated our marriage. I do believe that I was the only woman that he ever loved. Still, I feel that he was a horrible, selfish person to marry me knowing who he was and keeping that a secret from me.

"I told him that I wanted a divorce but he desperately wanted to keep the marriage intact. He suggested that we both keep his secret and maintain separate lives. I think that he was worried that if he came out of the closet it would be detrimental to his career. And he didn't want our friends and children to know.

"Of course, I could not go on with the marriage. In addition to shattering me, the news devastated my boys. They were very embarrassed at the time because there were not many openly gay men in society. It was a very difficult thing at that time for a child to say to their friends that their mother or father is gay.

"Looking back, there were some signs that should have caught my attention. Now that I am married to a heterosexual man, I can see that the sex life that I had with Harvey wasn't as loving, emotional, sexual, or frequent as it should have been. And the fact that he often had to stay late at work even though his type of sales job didn't typically require late nights should have been a sign to me.

"To this day, I think that what Harvey did was incredibly selfish. He should never, never, never have gotten married."

Sandra and Harvey dated in the late fifties and married at the start of the next decade, a time when most of American society looked upon homosexual relationships as deviant. No wonder gay men married straight women. But times have changed, right? Apparently not that much. In 2005, divorce lawyers are still seeing many gay men and women who hid their true sexual preference from heterosexual spouses, or were in denial about their sexual inclinations at the time or their marriage.

Jan and Phil

In Jan's case, her husband, a Mormon, lied to her for years about his double life in the gay world. Their story is compelling, because it shows how a straight spouse can be in denial about a spouse's true sexual preference for many years.

Jan and Phil met in the disco era of the late seventies. An outgoing eighteen-year-old, Jan intentionally knocked into the handsome Phil with her purse to get his attention. Her plot worked. A year and a half after ramming him with her bag, Jan married the twenty-year-old Phil in the Mormon Church where they took an oath to be married "for all time and eternity." This is what Jan told me about her twenty-five-year marriage to a gay man.

"Everything was great at the beginning of our marriage. We connected on many different levels. We were very good friends, and he was sweet and attentive. I think that he was attracted to me because I am very outgoing and he is a little quieter. He was tall, dark, and handsome. We both left college to start our married life. He managed an upscale jewelry store in town and I worked at first as a file clerk in an accounting office. Everything was wonderful at the beginning. I thought our sex life was great and we had the first of our three children on our second wedding anniversary. We bought a small house and I worked so that he could finish school and get a degree."

When I asked Jan if there were any signs at all of his interest in men at the beginning of her marriage she said this:

"There were signs, but I didn't focus on them. This may sound strange, but even in college I noticed that he did not carry his books in the same way that the other guys did. He sort of let them rest on his hip. But the first real sign, a sign that I ignored, occurred when we went together to purchase a dirty magazine. I had never seen as much as a *Playboy* magazine growing up and my husband was just amazed by that. He insisted that we go together to look at some. We went to a store, and looked at a few. My curiosity was quickly satisfied. But my husband wanted to buy one. He bought a magazine that was filled with only men involved in sex. I didn't think much about it at the time. However, a couple of months later I caught him masturbating to the magazine. He was very nonchalant about it. Looking back, that should have been a wake up call to me, but I was very naïve and did not know anything about homosexual behavior at the time.

"There were many other clues over the next several years of our marriage. Because he was very good looking, guys would come on to him, and when that occurred he would always pretend to be very annoyed. At the same time, he would frequently leave for a couple of hours at a time with no good explanation for the fifty miles he had put on his car. Sometimes men would call our house, ask for him, and suddenly he would have to leave for the office. When he came back he would frequently brush his teeth or change his clothes and put his dirty clothes in the hamper. Once I found a phone number in his wallet of a man who lived in town who was openly gay. When I asked him straight out if he were having a relationship with him, he become absolutely incensed with me that I could possibly think that he was gay. Because our sex life was still good, I began to think that I was the one with the problem. He really made me feel like I was unjustifiably paranoid.

"After we were married fifteen years, Phil finally admitted to going to gay bars, because he thought 'they were funny' and he 'enjoyed the attention' he received. Still, he consistently and adamantly denied that he was gay.

"There was one other important factor in all of this. When we had been married for seven years, he told me that when he was ten years old, he had been sexually molested by two brothers that lived down the street from him. He never told his parents, and although it had happened twenty years ago, he felt very victimized by this. I begged, and begged him to get counseling to help him get over it, but he always refused. Many times during our marriage, I suggested that we get individual or joint counseling, but he wouldn't hear of it.

"At this point in our marriage, there were a lot of other issues that we argued about. He rarely spent time with our kids. He was very focused on maintaining his appearance and had not advanced in his career. The burden of supporting our family fell to me. I constantly worked and did everything for our kids and around the house. I looked like an overweight 90-year-old woman because of the stress while he looked like Malibu Ken. I began questioning whether or not I should stay in the marriage.

"I know that this will sound unbelievable, but we shared a bedroom for twenty years before I really accepted the fact that Phil was gay. I think it finally sunk in when I started to find perverse S&M gay men's magazines barely hidden at the bottom of the trashcan. Finally, I woke up and realized that I was putting my life in danger every time we were intimate. I told him that I wanted him out. Instead, he just moved onto the couch. It was unbelievable, but he was still adamant that he never actually engaged in sex acts with men.

"Many times during our marriage Phil would go through depressions and take anti-depressants. Whenever I threatened to leave the marriage, he always told me how I would never make it on my own with the kids, and I stupidly believed him.

"Keep in mind that during this time, our community and our families had no idea. I didn't talk to anyone about this, and everyone thought we were a so-called perfect couple. I hate to say this but during the last terrible years of our marriage, I honestly wished that he would just die. I would secretly hope that he would get in a car accident I was so tired of it all.

"We finally decided to separate for a couple of months. During this time, I was so happy that I stopped my nervous eating and lost fifty pounds. That made it a lot easier to actually file the divorce papers. It was not until after we were divorced that Phil admitted everything I came to know. He had led a double life during our marriage and had engaged in more gay relationships than he could count.

"I thought that once Phil felt free to pursue an openly gay life that he would be happy. That is not what happened. After our divorce, he got very involved with drugs and alcohol, and become very uninvolved with our children, which has been extremely painful for them. Once my kids found out about Phil, they were angry at me for staying with him for so many years. They were absolutely shocked and devastated because, like the rest of our community, they had assumed that we had a great marriage. They had never heard us fight.

"I never give up hoping that Phil will find some happiness and turn his life around, but so far, that hasn't happened. I, on the other hand, feel like a new person."

Interesting Fact: In *My Husband is Gay* author Carol Grever cites a study by Dr. Raj Persaud, a psychiatrist at Maudsley Hospital in England, concerning the age that a married man comes to terms with his homosexuality. Dr. Persaud found two main patterns, both of which depend on social class. For men with lower incomes and status, homosexual activity frequently peaks during the late teens or early twenties, and then declines thereafter. Gay, married, upper-class men typically increase their homosexual activities as they grow older. Dr. Persaud theorized that poorer gays are most attractive to gay men in their youth, and their options declined as they aged and lost their youthful attractiveness. Older upper class men, on the other hand, have wealth to attract younger men, and more opportunities to travel.

Moving On

The vast majority of people who learn that their spouse is gay want a divorce. A marriage between a heterosexual spouse and a gay spouse is probably the ultimate example of a marriage where the parties have grown irretrievably apart. And where some people are able to go on with their marriage, most are not. Many people, however, benefit from individual therapy.

As far as children are concerned, learning that one parent is gay is no easy thing. Young children may benefit from one of the books listed below. No matter how you personally feel about a spouse that has come out of the closet, under no circumstances should you bad mouth the spouse or make derogatory comments about their sexual preference to your children.

Support:

Straight Spouse Network:
Address: 8215 Terrace Drive, El Cerrito, CA 94530-3058
(510) 525-0200
www.ssnetwk.org

Children of Lesbians and Gays Everywhere (COLAGE)
3543 18th Street, #17, San Francisco, CA 94110
(415) 861-5437
www.colage.org

Books:

My Husband is Gay: A Woman's Survival Guide
By Carol Grever, The Crossing Press, 2001

The Other Side of the Closet: The Coming-Out Crisis For Straight Spouses and

Families
By Amity Pierce Buxton, PhD, Wiley, 1994
Families Like Mine: Children of Gay Parents Tell It Like It Is
By Abigail Garner, HarperCollins, 2004

How It Feels To Have a Gay Or Lesbian Parent: A Book by Kids For Kids Of All Ages
By Judith Snow, Harrington Park Press, 2004

The Key Points

- Most couples grow apart inadvertently. They think that they can push the marriage cruise control button and the rest will take care of itself. It doesn't work that way. Couples grow apart when they become so involved with their children, their work, or their hobbies, that they don't make time for their spouse in their busy life. Marriage at a young age or a marriage between partners of significantly different ages also can cause the couple to grow apart. A change in goals or values, opposite personalities, and vast differences in social and intellectual development also cause spouses to drift in different directions.

- Atlanta attorney Elizabeth Lindsey told me that for a marriage to last, the couple has to develop a common history. "They need to develop stories together about their life," she said. I think this is a great way to think about it. If you and your spouse are driving on the same freeway but going in different directions, you are ultimately going to end up in completely different locations.

- Now that you know how a marriage grows apart, you can be vigilant in protecting yours from this insidious cause of divorce.

NINE
DIVORCE SYMPTOM #9:
LACK OF COMMITMENT

"If I could wave a magic wand to lessen the divorce rate, it would be to strengthen the sense of commitment that we make to marriage as an institution."
Patricia Ferrari, New York, NY

"As people are walking down the aisle they think, "Hey, if it doesn't work out I can just get divorced."
Jacqueline Whisnant, Newport Beach, CA

❖

Phoenix attorney Sheldon Mitchell told me about a recent conversation that he had with a client that summed up the lack of commitment to marriage that is all too common in American culture today. His wealthy, middle-aged client mentioned in passing that she was traveling to San Francisco that weekend to attend her daughter's wedding. When Mitchell inquired whether she was happy with her daughter's choice of a mate, his client responded, "Yes, it is fine for a first marriage."

This blasé attitude toward divorce was unheard of just a generation ago. Lucy and Ricky had marital problems galore and Fred and Ethel's marriage rarely sizzled, but divorce was never suggested. For the *I Love Lucy* gang, it was as if ending a marriage wasn't an option once you were in one. Flash forward one television generation to the mega hit *Friends*. Ross, a lead character on the show, is divorced three times over the course of the ten-year series and no one blinks.

Many, many, many of the divorce attorneys that I spoke to cited the average American's general lack of commitment to the institution of marriage as a large reason why one out of two marriages don't go the distance. They described clients who recited marital vows with imaginary fingers crossed behind their backs. The bride and groom may have been saying "I do," but they were thinking "I might."

Several of the divorced people that I interviewed told me that they had serious doubts about their future spouse before the wedding date but felt that the "train had already left the station." Many of these people conceded that they mistakenly thought that it would be easier to go through with the ceremony and obtain a divorce if things did not work out, than to phone guests with the news that the wedding was off.

Where does this lack of commitment come from? After all, it wasn't that many years ago that "till death do us part," meant exactly that. The lawyers that I spoke to blamed the western world's commitment problem on two things.

One is our societal compulsion to replace things the moment a newer model becomes available. Functioning computers, cell phones, and cars are immediately replaced the moment a newer model becomes available. Add to this obsession with obtaining the latest and the newest to our change in attitudes toward our careers. Workers no longer strive to obtain the proverbial gold watch for a lifetime of service to a single company. Instead, they hop from company to company leaving their former colleagues and tasks behind without a second thought when something better presents itself. So perhaps it should come as no surprise that when we are tired of the challenges presented by our marriages, our thoughts immediately drift to the benefits that a newer (or richer, or funnier, or better looking) spouse might provide.

Our legal system was also blamed for discouraging marital commitment. Many divorce attorneys noted that our laws make it both too easy to marry and too easy to divorce. I discuss this later, but for now consider how little our government requires for a marriage license.

My home state's prerequisites to marriage are typical in their simplicity. In California, you can enter into marriage, probably the most powerful and life altering legal contract that you will ever make, at the age of eighteen (or younger if a parent agrees) for about seventy bucks. You do need to go to the trouble of locating a witness but even there the state doesn't want to make things too difficult.

According to the Department of California Health Service's website, the observer you select to witness this tremendous legal commitment need only be "old enough to know that they are witnessing a marriage ceremony, and be able to sign their name on the official marriage license." I'm not an expert on this, but it looks like your witness could be a six-year-old child who knows both how to sign their name, and understands that a fancy dress, a nice suit, and a long kiss signify that a marriage has occurred. (California is not lax about all of the licenses that it grants its residents. A lifetime hunting license currently costs $609.00 and requires ten hours of specialized training).

Is a lack of commitment threatening your marriage? At the end of this section, look for a series of questions under the heading "Is the Grass Greener?" designed to weed out whether or not your attitude toward marriage in general evidences a lack of commitment. But before we get there, it is important to understand how and why divorce went from being a social negative to something that is celebrated with friends at "divorce showers." How did our marriage vows go from sacred commitments to tentative maybes in just one generation?

Interesting Fact: In response to criticism from many pro-marriage groups over the government's failure to require more of its citizens before they can marry and divorce, three states— Arizona, Arkansas, and Louisiana—now offer newlyweds the option of entering into a "covenant marriage." Unlike a run of the mill marriage which is both easy to obtain and easy to end, a covenant marriage requires the couple to obtain pre-marital counseling before they exchange rings. Divorces are only available on fault grounds; commission of a felony by a spouse, adultery, abuse, and long periods of separation. Additional counseling is required before a divorce is granted.

The public has been slow to sign up for these marriages. For example in Arkansas, 37,942 marriage licenses were issued in 2002, but only sixty-seven couples signed up for the covenant marriage option. And just twenty-four who were already married converted their regular marriages to covenant marriages.

The Way We Were

"Some people hang in there come hell or high water. And other people, you look at them funny and they are out of there." Burt Dart, Salt Lake City, UT

Atlanta attorney Ned Bates told me a great story about the state of marriage in the late 1890's in Georgia that shows how far we have come as a society in accepting divorce. It seems that if you were miserably married in Georgia at the turn of the last century, your only option was to petition the state legislature for a divorce. At the time, Georgia's local courts had no power to grant divorces. When the third person petitioned the Georgia legislature for a divorce in a single year, the legislature expressed exasperation at their state's high rate of divorce. In the late 19th century and early 20th century, divorce was not only unheard of in Georgia, but in most every other part of the country as well.

Divorce is so common today that it is hard to imagine that it once had a negative stigma attached to it. Ask anyone over sixty years old, and they will tell you that when they were young, society had a highly negative view of divorce. I interviewed many women and men for this book who were first married in the 1950s who mentioned that at that time divorce was not even a thought when they walked down the aisle. The few people they had heard of (most didn't know anyone personally) who had been divorced were generally looked upon as social aberrations. But then things began to change in a big way.

Societal Changes: How America Went From "We" to "Me":

"We now have a culture in the United States where we tend to immediately think of divorce when things go wrong, and, of course, at some point things will go wrong."Mary Wechsler, Seattle, WA

Marriage is a "we" thing. So it is not surprising that when Americans went from "we" to "me" in the late sixties and early seventies, divorce rates began to skyrocket. Suddenly, marriage went from being a social convention where individual happiness was a windfall, to an institution that was dependent on a lifetime of personal happiness for its survival. Stephanie Coontz in her recent book *Marriage, a History* summarized this important change this way, "The more people hoped to achieve personal happiness within marriage, the more critical they became of empty or unsatisfying relationships."

It wasn't only our increased narcissism that caused divorce to lose its stigma. Smart women entering the workplace in droves put a strain on both their marriage and the marriages of other women. Now, women didn't necessarily need a man financially. And bright, ambitious men who had previously had very few workplace options when it came to having affairs, started to work side by side with tempting women who were also bright, attractive, and ambitious.

In a very short period of time historically speaking, our female role model went from Ozzie's wife Harriet (who appeared to happily clean her home and take care of her children while wearing a dress and pantyhose), to the career minded Mary Tyler Moore. In 1963, feminist author Betty Friedan added more fuel to the fire, telling trapped housewives that it was okay to feel dissatisfied with their lot, in her groundbreaking book *The Feminine Mystique.*

One's commitment to personal happiness began to trump the commitment they had made to their spouse. While this may have been a welcome change in cases where husbands or wives had suffered silently while their spouses wrecked the family finances through gambling or spending addictions, suffered verbal or physical abuse, or lived in a marriage that was marred by drug or alcohol abuse, it also gave rise to flushing marriages simply because they no longer radiated honeymoon level heat. The idea that good marriages are built with a lot of mutual effort and patience started to take a backseat for people who were quickly getting used to instant gratification.

Nearly every divorce lawyer that I spoke to lamented the fact that people seem to be leaving their marriages for reasons that are increasingly trivial. As Atlanta divorce attorney Shiel Edlin sees it, "The threshold of what gets people to pull the trigger has gone down over the last twenty years. People are more self-absorbed than ever before, more pleasure seeking, willing to accept less pain, and basically looking for instant gratification. The notion of being committed is lost among most Americans."

The irony about our commitment issues is that while we have trouble keeping our marital commitments, we seem to have no trouble making them in the first place. Manhattan attorney Patricia Ferrari pointed out that even when her clients were in the throes of the most horrific and painful splits imaginable, they clung to the hope that there still was a potential soul-mate out there for them with whom they could marry and live happily ever after. Many attorneys commented that in cases where it was the husband pulling the divorce trigger, wife number two (or three) was already lined up. Statistics confirm that lack of commitment to one marriage doesn't evidence a lack of commitment to the institution of marriage. More than seventy-five percent of people who get divorced ultimately get remarried and they do it fairly quickly. The median number of years people wait to remarry after their first divorce is just over three years.

Legal Changes

"It is too easy to get a divorce." Mel Frumkes, Miami, FL

As Brittany Spears demonstrated with her drunken wouldn't-it-be-funny-if-we-got-married Las Vegas wedding, getting married in this country is a piece of cake. But it is not only weddings that are technically easy to obtain. Contrary to what you might think, obtaining a divorce, from a strictly legal standpoint, is quite simple as well. In cases where there is not a lot of property to divide and custody or spousal support issues are not relevant, it is usually just a matter of filing the appropriate paperwork and paying the filing fees.

The days when a spouse had to prove that the other party was at fault before a court would dissolve the marriage are ancient legal history. In 1970, California adopted no fault divorce and, to some extent, nearly every state in the Union ultimately followed California's lead. In some states, fault is still relevant for determining the distribution of the couple's property or setting the amount of spousal support, but the divorce itself is typically no fault.

Chicago attorney Steven Lake pointed out how changes in our legal system have made divorce easy and in many cases, downright tempting. "Divorce has taken on a life of its own. There is no stigma to divorce anymore. The marriage contract seems to be the only legal contract that you can break without suffering any legal consequences like damages."

Recent changes in custody laws have also had the unintended side effect of making divorce more attractive to men. With more and more states rejecting the old model of custody to mom and every other weekend with dad, fathers no longer have to choose between their children and freedom from their marriage. This new custody arrangement also provides a financial windfall where the father is the primary breadwinner. In most states, the more custodial time the father has, the lower the child support obligation.

No wonder then that America has seemingly stopped associating marriage with commitment. It is as if our legal system conspired with social changes to make divorce both extremely acceptable and accessible.

Interesting Fact: Many family law attorneys and social commentators pin some of the blame for our high divorce rates on the adoption of no fault divorce statutes. Ironically, the change from fault to no fault came out of recommendations made by a California task force that was formed to find ways to reduce the incidence of divorce. The Governor's Commission on the Family was initially formed in 1966 to begin a "concerted assault on the high incidence of divorce in our society and its often tragic consequences." In addition to overhauling California's existing divorce laws, the Commission was charged with the duty to "determine the feasibility of developing significant and meaningful courses in family life education, to be offered in the public schools."

The Commission recommended "that the existing fault grounds of divorce and the concept of technical fault as a determinant in the division of community property, support and alimony be eliminated, and that marital dissolution be permitted only upon a finding that the marriage has irreparably failed, after penetrating scrutiny and after the parties have been given by the judicial process every resource in aid of reconciliation."

What actually took place? The Commission's findings were only enacted in part. Fault grounds were eliminated, but there is no "penetrating judicial scrutiny" by the court into whether or not a marriage has "irreparably failed." In fact, the only scrutinizing by the court is into whether or not the parties checked the box labeled "irreconcilable differences." As for providing "every resource in aid of reconciliation," there are no resources provided whatsoever.

What about the Commission's duty to study the possibility of offering "family life education" courses in public schools? Ironically, the Commission's report reserved that issue for "future study." More than forty years have passed since the Commission made its report and California does not require courses in family life education.

The Grass is Greener Phenomenon

"Many clients get divorced because they think that somewhere else the grass is greener. After spending a lot of time in this business I can tell you that the grass is not greener." Steven Briggs, Newport Beach, CA

"One of my clients said to me after her third marriage ended, 'I wish I had listened to you and stayed with my first husband.'" Sharon Corbitt, Tulsa, OK

I live in Los Angeles where celebrities change spouses about as often as they change their underwear. Although I only listed a single name under the "grass is greener" quote above, more than half of the lawyers that I spoke to complained that many of their clients left marriages that were imperfect but improvable because they bought into the grass is greener fantasy.

So what is the answer to the million-dollar question? Is the grass really greener elsewhere? Usually not. The grass may be different elsewhere but it will probably not be greener. There will be weeds that need to be pulled in your next marriage; different weeds for sure, but weeds nonetheless. Both statistics and anecdotal evidence bears this out.

As you saw in Chapter 7, second marriages fail at an even higher rate than first marriages. Plus, every single divorce lawyer that I interviewed felt that where a client with children at home left a lackluster marriage solely because he or she thought that the grass was greener elsewhere, most of these people found out that they had been suffering under an illusion.

Miami attorney Andy Leinoff told me a story that suggests most people learn the hard way that the grass in their own marriage is just about as green as the grass in their neighbor's marriage. Leinoff represented a successful doctor who didn't feel appreciated by his wife. According to this doctor, his wife constantly pressured him to work harder, and make more money. A nurse who worked with him and lived in an apartment started to tell the doctor how wonderful, smart, and successful he was. He absolutely couldn't believe it! His wife had told him just the opposite for many years. The punch line? The doctor marries the nurse, she quits her job, and after a few years asks him why he isn't making more money.

And Los Angeles attorney Stacy Phillips commented on a grass is greener trend that she sees frequently: "What I see all too often is that while the wife is home raising the kids, the husband meets someone at work who seems to share his interests. Husband divorces wife #1 to marry wife #2 and wife #2 promptly quits her job and stays home.

Leinoff's and Phillip's clients got different grass, not greener grass.

The Grass is Greener Quiz:

Do you suffer from the grass is greener illusion? Look at the following statements. Do they reflect the way that you think about your marriage?

- I frequently find my spouse boring. If I were married to someone else, I would mostly find that other person exciting and interesting.
- My spouse is not as attractive as when I married him/her. If I were married to someone else, they would always be attractive to me.
- My spouse nags me about trivial things. If I were married to someone else, they would accept me for who I am and they wouldn't nag me.
- My spouse and I have nothing in common except for the kids. If I were married to someone else, we would do everything together.
- My spouse is always working. If I were married to someone else, they wouldn't work hard and I would have the same lifestyle that I do now.
- When I was young, single, and childless, many smart, attractive people were interested in dating me. Even though I am older now, and the parent of three children, these same types of people would be available to me.
- My husband/wife doesn't appreciate me. The people I chat with on the internet continually tell me how wonderful I am. I would like to remarry someone like that.
- When my husband/wife and I first married, we couldn't get enough of each other sexually. Now, we have sex about twice a month. If I were married to someone else, we would be having sex all the time.

Is There a Cure For Lack of Commitment?

"Divorce lawyers tend to stay married for a very long time because we know how awful divorce is. Most people believe in the myth that it is easier to get divorced than to fix their marriage. Divorce lawyers know better." Sandra Morgan Little, Albuquerque, NM

Up until this point, I have been able to make suggestions on how you can cure most every symptom of divorce. Money problems, sex issues, communication troubles all fixable when they are tackled early on. Although I knew that lack of commitment would have to be identified as a major symptom of divorce, I dreaded writing about it because it felt like it was a divorce symptom without a fix. I believed that if you and your spouse had children at home and still felt that leaving your marriage and starting over with someone else would be easier than dealing with the problems in your marriage head-on, that there was little that I could say that would change your mind. Then it occurred to me. If you could have a sneak preview of your divorce and its aftermath, maybe you might think twice before giving up on your marriage.

Many of the divorce attorneys that I spoke to mentioned that being in the unique position to see the reality of divorce has made their own marriages stronger. Despite working in a career that can take a huge toll on one's own emotions and time, many of the divorce lawyers that I interviewed felt that their work helped them not only stay married, but taught them how to have good marriages. Here is what they know about divorce and what you don't.

The Truth About The Divorce Process

"Many people have no idea what divorce is like. They think that divorce is the solution to the problems in their lives. Many people realize after a year or two that divorce wasn't the solution but by then it is too late." Jacqueline Whisnant, Newport Beach, CA

There is no doubt that having a divorce lawyer for a parent shaped my views on marriage. Working as a family law attorney distorted my perceptions even further. After I attended a particularly hostile deposition where the parties seethed on opposite sides of the long conference table, I announced to my family and friends that I had devised a foolproof husband screening strategy. Convinced that people would do the work to stay married if they had witnessed the pain and anger of divorce firsthand, I vowed that if I ever was in a relationship with someone that I wanted to marry, I would insist that my potential fiancée sit through a week of divorce proceedings at our county courthouse.

My strategy was not original, just the application was. "Scared Straight" programs already existed where at risk youths were taken on tours of jails to disabuse them of any notions that they might have about the realities of incarceration. Although I never put Wendy's "Too Scared To Divorce Plan" into action, I always felt that if people had a divorce crystal ball, they would think twice, or three times, before walking down the divorce road.

Misconceptions About Divorce

"Many of my clients have said after the divorce that it was a mistake." Lawrence Stotter, San Francisco, CA

St. Louis attorney Allen Zerman told me a great story that shows how little the general public knows about how the divorce process works. Zerman's client, a woman who was entitled to receive approximately half of an estate worth literally hundreds of millions of dollars, was elated when her manicurist told her a divorce "trick." The woman had followed her manicurist's suggestion to take a check from the back of her checkbook, write a $10,000 check to "cash" and then hide the money. No doubt her $10,000 "secret" ultimately cost her far more in litigation costs because now her husband had reason to suspect that she had a habit of "hiding" marital property.

The problem according to Zerman, is that the public's perception of the rules of divorce are frequently formed by stories they have heard from their friends, barbers, and manicurists. So far, there are no reality television shows that follow a contested divorce from start to finish. The only way to really understand what happens in a divorce is to go through one yourself. Here is the hard truth about divorce.

The Trauma of Divorce

"People don't realize how emotional and demeaning the process is and the process is demeaning." Lowell Sucherman, San Francisco, CA

South Carolina attorney Ken Lester told me that most people are not emotionally prepared for the trauma of contested divorces. While he recommends to his clients that they work with a therapist to help them through the emotional trials of the process, he notes that part of what makes divorce so difficult is that most everything a client believes in has been shattered by the ending of the marriage. "When a marriage falls apart people start questioning their ability to make decisions. This frequently causes difficult problems with the case because it makes clients doubt and question all of their decision making," he said.

Why is divorce so traumatic? In addition to the emotional despair that comes with ending a marriage, the process itself is frequently very demeaning. Every single dollar that you made and spent during your marriage is open to scrutiny by your attorney, your spouse's attorney, a court reporter, a secretary or two, possibly a paralegal, and a judge. If you and your spouse can't agree on a custody arrangement, your competency as a parent will be questioned and analyzed by strangers. Nearly everything that you thought was private is exposed.

The following is a partial list of information and documents that you would likely be required to provide as part of a contested divorce:

- Copies of your tax returns
- Every single cancelled check for at least the last couple of years
- Copies of every single recurring bill
- A copy of your will or trust
- 1099 and/or W-2 forms
- If you own a business, every document that bears on the income earned from your business
- Statements from retirement and pension plans
- Life insurance statements and policies
- Statements from all savings accounts, checking accounts, money market accounts, and certificates of deposit
- Documents relating to personal and/or business loans

- Appraisals of real and personal property
- Appraisals of businesses

Divorce and Your Kids

"Divorce is generally a time when you learn a lot about yourself and it is not all good. Frequently people get narcissistic, and the kid's feelings get left out. This doesn't occur because the person is not a good parent but because the parent becomes overwhelmed by what they are going through." Ellen Widen Kessler, New Orleans, LA

Many family law attorneys won't handle contested custody cases, because they are very difficult emotionally. While sometimes they are necessary because "there are parents who are dreadful and should not have open access to their children," in most cases it is better for the child to have both parents involved in their lives. As one attorney put it, "Children typically yearn for both parents."

Still, bitter parents can't seem to stop criticizing the other parent in front of their children, or resist the temptation of using their child as a messenger. Kessler told me a story that epitomizes the types of things that parents do to put their children in the middle. A client of hers (who she stopped representing because of her reprehensible conduct) was certain that her soon to be ex-husband had another women in his life. She instructed her child to go through his father's drawers to hunt for any evidence that would confirm her suspicions. Clearly this woman put her own interests before the best interests of her child.

Then there are the parents who too quickly try to merge their newest love with children who are still reeling from the break-up of their parents. Couple this with hurt ex-spouses who try to seek revenge by making false allegations against the other spouse with the hope of distancing their children from that parent. In all of these types of cases it is clear who the real losers are. It is the very rare couple that can split with each other, and put their children's interests first every time and all the time.

The Truth About Life After Divorce

"In divorce cases where the people are angry or vindictive it is because they are trying to get compensation for the wrongs of the marriage; that is why people will destroy proper-ty before they will let it go to the other party. Our clients don't fight because of the value of the property. They fight because it is their way of addressing perceived wrongs from the marriage and to punish the other party." Edward Winer, Minneapolis, MN

"People get divorced because they are unhappy and they think that by getting divorced that their life will totally turn around. Does it? No. For some people it does, but for most people it is the same or worse." Bob Nachshin, Santa Monica, CA

I asked Palm Beach family law attorney Lewis Kapner what he felt were the most common misconceptions about life after divorce. Here is his list.

Divorce Myth #1: "I will be better off financially after the divorce."

You don't need to have a degree in accounting to figure out that two can live a lot cheaper than one. In the typical divorce, one mortgage or rent payment becomes two. Property tax, electric bills, and water bills start to come in pairs. A new household requires new furniture, a second set of clothing for children, and new appliances.

Divorce Myth #2: "Friends and family will take my side."

Many people wrongly assume that when they inform their friends and rela-tives about their spouse's reprehensible behavior (especially when there has been an affair) that they will be viewed as "the hero", and their social group will discard their spouse, "the chump." This rarely is the case.

Divorce Myth #3: "Our divorce will be easy. We will just divide up all of our stuff."

People who suffer from a "divorce is no big deal" mentality are typically surprised by how long the process takes and how much it costs. People are shocked by the accountants and documents that are required even when the divorce is relatively amicable. Plus, they underestimate the human dynamic. "Divorce is not like two college roommates going their own way after college is over. When you inject the high degree of emotional betrayal that people feel, people don't act the way that you would necessarily expect."

And I will add one more misconception about divorce to Kapners' list:

Divorce Myth #4: If you have kids, divorce will get your spouse out of your house, but not out of your life.

Thanks to the father's rights movement, the increased involvement by dads in their children's lives, and a change in judicial attitudes, good fathers who live close to their children are no longer relegated to every other weekend visitation. Those days are gone for good in most states.

What does that mean for you? If you and your spouse have a child in common, your spouse will continue to be in your life on a regular basis. (And thanks to email and cell phones, more than you could have ever imagined ten years ago!)

A family law attorney named Anita Wyzanski Robboy wrote a book called, *Aftermarriage: The Myth of Divorce-Unspoken Marriage Agreements and Their Impact on Divorce*. Here is what she had to say about Divorce Myth #4:

"Unfortunately, the [divorce decree] is not a ticket out of the obligations and duties of marriage. Little will really change as a result of the divorce, and certainly far less than many had hoped. As one family court judge always tells parties at the close of their [divorce] hearing, 'You are no longer husband and wife, but you are parents forever.'

"Nearly every divorcing person has the fantasy that his or her partner will be shed. Persons who have had long marriages or marriages with children will never be able to shed their partners like a chrysalis. They will have a thousand points of connection in the future because of their children, their financial obligations to each other, and their history."

My favorite part of Robboy's observation is her conclusion: "In effect, all that the divorce process really can do is rearrange the place of the 'other' in their lives…"

Minneapolis attorney Edward Winer summed up the dramatic effect of divorce: "People can assume that divorce will impact every single aspect of their life. It is literally like having the rug pulled our from under you. Divorce affects who your friends are, your relationship with in-laws, how much money you will have, your seats to sporting and cultural events, and your relationship with your children."

The Key Points

- Divorce is very expensive.
- Most people's standard of living is negatively effected when they divorce.
- Divorce is very difficult emotionally.
- Most parents can't resist the temptation of bad-mouthing the other parent, or putting their children in the middle during and after a divorce.
- Your friends and family will not automatically take "your side" when you get divorced.
- Many people will have access to all of your financial information and spending habits when you divorce.
- The grass will be different with another spouse, but you will still have to work on your marriage.

TEN
WHY MARRIAGE MATTERS

"The more divorce work that I do, the more I respect the good marriages when I see them. The greatest gift in the world is a good marriage, and the biggest disaster is a bad marriage."
Donn Fullenweider, Houston, TX

❖

Marriage matters. According to even the most recent studies, the goal of most Americans is to have a happy marriage. Even the generation of kids who grew up in a society where divorce is seen as "no big deal" want to be married someday. In a 1992 study of goals of high-school seniors, "having a good marriage and family life" was their number one aspiration.

But perhaps the best evidence that marriage is a social construct that has a huge appeal to humans is that with one exception, there is a culture of marriage in every single society in the world. Stephanie Coontz, the author of *Marriage, A History*, writes: "We know of only once society in world history that did not make marriage a central way of organizing social and personal life, the Na people of China. With that exception, marriage has been, in one form or another, a universal social institution throughout recorded history."

I'm guessing that if you are reading this book, you don't need to be convinced that marriage in general matters, just that marriage to the one you're with matters. It does matter, especially if you have children together.

Studies on the consequences of divorce on children show everything from a higher probability that they will follow in their parents' divorce footsteps when it comes to their own marriages to a lower probability that they will attend a prestigious college. Not swayed by statistics? Then consider the overwhelming amount of anecdotal evidence on the pain that divorce causes to the parents of those children.

I asked one freshly divorced father how he felt when he first saw his ex-wife with another man. "Seeing my ex with another man wasn't easy, but when I saw that man buckle my two-year-old son into his car seat it was devastating." Another divorced father described the pain he felt when he learned that his ex-wife was trying to turn their daughter against him to punish him for leaving her. "My daughter, who is the greatest light in my life, told me that her mother had told her that I had wanted a boy instead of her. My daughter asked me, 'Why didn't you want me daddy?'"

Let me be absolutely clear on one thing. There are some circumstances when divorce is better than marriage for parents and their children. Where there is physical or emotional abuse in the home, divorce is frequently warranted. Drug and alcohol abuse and gambling addictions frequently make divorce unavoidable. And in what the experts call "high conflict" marriages (which account for less than one-third of all divorce cases), divorce is frequently better for the children than continuing with the marriage. But in the majority of cases, it is nearly always better for everyone in the family if parents can fix their marital problems and stay together.

One divorce attorney from Denver thought it would be interesting to conduct a study where people would be asked ten years after their divorce if they were sorry that they didn't stay in the marriage and work on their problems. After several years in the divorce business, she felt that many people would say that they wished that they had tried harder to make their marriage work. Many attorneys told me stories about people who came to their office who were sitting on the divorce fence and decided not to divorce after discussing their marital problems with the attorney. Others told me about clients who remarried a spouse after finding out they were no happier divorced. Contrary to what you might think, the divorce attorneys that I interviewed all derived a lot of personal satisfaction when they felt that they had a hand in helping a marriage stay together.

If you are experiencing marriage problems and wondering if the work that it takes to make a good marriage is worth it, consider the following findings that were reported by marriage researchers Linda J. Waite and Maggie Gallagher in their book *The Case For Marriage: Why Married People Are Happier, Healthier, and Better Off Financially:*

- on average, children of married parents are physically and mentally healthier, better educated, and ultimately enjoy more career and marital success
- on average, divorce causes a child's standard of living to be reduced by one-third because children of divorce do not have the time, attention, or social resources of two parents
- father/child relationships frequently diminish over time where the father does not share custody
- children in step families and single parent families are more likely to experiment with cigarettes, alcohol, and marijuana
- children of divorce are nearly twice as likely to engage in sex at an early age

Does this mean that your choice is between an unhappy marriage and happy kids? The most important statistic is yet to come. According to a poll conducted by marriage researcher Linda Waite, 86% of couples who reported their marriage as "unhappy," but stuck it out, later reported an improvement in their marriages with three-fifths reporting five years later that their marriages were "quite happy" or "very happy." Waite concluded that: "Permanent marital unhappiness is surprisingly rare among the couples who stick it out."

For those of you with school-age children who think that getting a divorce and starting over is easier than trying to fix your marriage, remember this: Divorce will get your spouse out of your house, but it will not get your spouse out of your life.

If you were a stay-at-home parent and you and your spouse do not have substantial assets, you will be dependent on your spouse for a time for money. And, if you are the only one in your family working, your state of residence may require a significant portion of your assets to be paid to your former spouse for several years. Unless you are extremely wealthy, both of your lifestyles will take a hit as it is obviously a lot more expensive to run two households than one.

Your ex will not disappear. You will continue to see him or her at the little league field and at school functions. If you live in a state that promotes shared custody, you will likely spend your child's birthday with them only every other year. Ditto for Christmas and Thanksgiving.

Your former spouse will continue to be in your life through your child. You will see them when you drop off your child or pick up your child. You will exchange numerous emails and phone calls with your ex as you try to juggle your children's schedule with both of yours.

Iris Krasnow wrote a great book called *Surrendering To Marriage: Husbands, Wives, and Other Perfections*. After interviewing dozens of people who had been divorced and remarried someone else, she comes to the conclusion that although life is different in a second marriage, the challenges of stepchildren and the ghosts of ex-spouses do not necessarily mean life is better. Her conclusion? You might as well love the one you're with. Krasnow explained, "...[W]hat you often get with someone you believed to be smarter and sexier are even bigger problems than the ones you left behind. This from dealing with stepchildren, ex-spouses, and the realization that the same tough issues are surfacing again, because you took your own imperfect self with you, and from that there is no escape."

If you bought this book, it is because you already know that living in a home with two emotionally healthy, happy parents is better for your children than commuting between two homes. And now you know how to recognize the symptoms of divorce. It is up to you to take those symptoms seriously, and to cure them.

THE DIVORCE LAWYERS' GUIDE TO **STAYING MARRIED**

ELEVEN
MARITAL ADVICE FROM DIVORCE ATTORNEYS

At the end of many of my interviews, I would ask this question: "What advice would you give to someone before they got married, or to someone who is already married, to help them stay married?" My question was frequently greeted by a chuckle or a large sigh, but the attorneys' responses were extremely insightful and sincere. Although some of the responses are similar, I still included them because it emphasizes how important certain issues are to making marriage work.

I have added the marital advice at the end of the book with the hope that you will read them often if you are married, read them before you remarry if you have been divorced, and, if you are considering marriage for the first time, take them to heart before you tie the knot.

Marriage is a very serious business. When you marry you enter into a very powerful legal contract. It is the biggest financial and personal transaction of your life. You need to look at the other person and realize that you are not going to change them. Ask yourself this: "Does this individual have the basic qualities that matter to me; characteristic traits that aren't going to change over time? It is not all about the cake, the wedding planner, your gifts and your dress. It takes a lot of work to make it work.
Mabry De Buys, Seattle, WA

Pay attention to the family of origin. This is everyone's role model of what a marriage looks like. And ask yourself if you will be able to trust this person with your medical care and money.
Steve Harhai, Denver, CO

Put the sexual attraction in its proper perspective. Don't be wowed by the physical attraction. You need to stop and think what it is going to be like when you each have an extra 20 pounds around your waists. Don't marry someone with the expectation that you will change the things that you don't like. Look to see how your prospective spouse's family expresses love.
Bill Hunnicut, Denver, CO

No one should get married under 30. When you are under 30 your expectations are immature concerning the real world. You haven't lived long enough to know the flavor of the world.
Marna Tucker, Washington, D.C.

There is a whole lack of knowledge about what makes a healthy marriage. Spouses need to deal early on with money, sex, in-laws, deciding who is going to raise the kids, and who is going to work. Or, if both spouses are going to go to work, they need to decide how they are going to share the responsibilities of the house.
Elizabeth Lindsay, Atlanta, GA

Marriage brings a lot of satisfaction to a person, especially if they plan on having children. Wait several years before you get married and don't marry young. Live together first to see if the day to day relationship works.
Maurice Kutner, Miami, FL

Marriage is hard work. The decision to marry should not be based on a single factor. People need to stop underestimating the importance of family relationships, and religious differences.
Marshall Wolf, Cleveland, OH

Your spouse should be your best friend and you need to treat them like they are your best friend.
Herb Palkovitz, Cleveland, OH

Take your time to get to know the person before you marry. You need to ask yourself: "Is this the person you want to walk on the beach with when your hands are wrinkled and you walk slow."
Steve Briggs, Newport Beach, CA

Never put being right ahead of the relationship. To do this, there are three phrases that you need to keep in mind and use frequently when you are communicating with your spouse: "You are right, good point, and that is interesting."
Jackie Whisnant, Newport Beach, CA

For a successful marriage, a couple should have many common goals, interests, desires and objectives. The couple should experience a lot of different things together before they commit to marriage. They need to know and understand each other's backgrounds because a person's family and the environment that they came out of can have a lot to do with their future relationships. People revert back to where they came from.
John Schilling, Newport Beach, CA

Get premarital counseling before the wedding. A good marriage counselor gets a couple to talk openly about their goals, and teaches them how to listen to the other person's problems.
David Sandor, Irvine, CA

Couples need to sit down with each other, a counselor, or a religious advisor and outline their general thoughts and feelings about whether to have children and how they will be raised with the caveat that things and feelings could change.

They need to discuss seemingly simple things like are you going to be mad if I have one night a week with my girlfriends, or if I have a monthly hunting weekend with the guys. It sounds trivial, but these are the kind of things that really cause problems in marriage. If it is not acceptable that your fiancé is going to be with his buddies once a month, than you

shouldn't get married. People tend to go into a marriage thinking that they are going to change their spouse, but that isn't going to happen.
Mary McCurley, Dallas, TX

There are three important rules to remember when selecting a mate: one, don't be rushed; two, be sure that your politics, religion, sexual interest, and values are all compatible, and three, make sure that you are in romantic love-not sister/brother love. If you don't have romantic love at the beginning you won't have it at the end.
Eric Spevak, Haddonfield, NJ

If you are of different religions or ethnic backgrounds, you need to discuss how those differences will impact your relationship. Have a candid discussion on how you will raise your kids. When people come in for a prenuptial agreement, I tell the couple to take a piece of paper, draw a line down the middle, and for each party to list their views on a variety of issues on either side of the line. Many people don't end up getting married after engaging in this exercise because they recognize that they are not compatible.
Herbert Glieberman, Chicago, IL

People pull the trigger way too fast. It is important to get beyond the honeymoon period before you get engaged. Go on vacations together. Live together. Experience many ups and downs together. Make sure that you know the person well and that you consider the person your closest friend.
Scott Weston, Santa Monica, CA

Be open and honest. If you are unhappy, let your spouse know it. Remember that a good argument is better than no argument at all. If people were open and honest with their spouses, fifty percent of divorces could be avoided.
Bernard Rinella, Chicago, IL

Before the wedding, both the man and woman should be as introspective as possible and think about both their strong and weak points. Then they need to share all of those strengths and weaknesses with each other. Both parties need to honestly consider whether or not they can deal with the other's weaknesses.

Stephen Arnold, Birmingham, AL

Give in early and often. If both parties keep giving in they will have a great relationship. Remember that if you leave this mate to find another mate, you still end up with another person who you will also have to compromise with.

Don Schiller, Chicago, IL

Before you marry, take a communication skills course of some sort like Pairs. (Practical Application of Intimate Relationship Skills, www.pairs.com)

Lynn Gold-Bikin, Norristown, PA

Marriage is the most important decision that an individual will make in their life because it affects nearly every aspect of life. The decision to marry has to be made carefully and thoughtfully. One of the most important things to learn about the other is whether you share similar goals and values.

James Feldman, Chicago, IL

In the marriages that make it, people don't say, "That isn't what I bargained for when I got married." When there is a change in the marriage, for example where the wife goes back to school, or the husband changes careers, the most important thing a spouse can do is be adaptable and support changes in the other spouse.

Patricia Ferrari, New York, NY

Before you get married find out if you feel the same way about children, money, and careers. Picking a good premarital class can be very helpful. And where one or both of the parties has significant assets, it is a good idea to get a prenuptial agreement because it eliminates the potential for arguments over those assets. There is no other enterprise involving money and

property where you wouldn't have a written document, and marriage should not be the exception to that rule.
Joanne Ross Wilder, Pittsburgh, PA

Wait until you are at least twenty-five years old before you marry. Under no circumstances should you get married any earlier. Take your marriage vows seriously. Grow together—up, down, or sideways; it doesn't matter as long as you grow together.
Herndon Inge, Mobile, AL

Check out the other side before you get married, specifically whether or not your intended was abused as a child, or he or she has a parent who is or was an alcoholic. In those cases, no matter how wonderful your love is, your potential spouse is like a car that that will run out of gas at a certain point. No matter how much you like them, move on.
Wolfgang Anderson, Seattle, WA

Before you get married—when you are still in love and think it is going to last forever--develop a communication system. If you do, you will have a much better chance of making a marriage that lasts.
Janet George, Seattle, WA

After you get married, choose couple friends who share the same values as you do and who value marriage and family.
JoAnn Reynolds, Portland, OR

Have marital discussions in the "I" form instead of the "You" form. Conversations that begin with "you never" aren't productive. Begin your sentences with "I feel." Don't speak about your spouse in "always" or "never" terms.
Helen Christian, Salt Lake City, UT

People court their lover, but not their spouse. Couples need to do the same thing for a husband or wife that they would do with a new girlfriend or

boyfriend. To keep the marriage alive, people need to keep surprises in the relationship.
Lowell Sucherman, San Francisco, CA

Couples need to be close together on how money will be handled and how kids are going to be raised. Where couples have different views on those subjects, it will affect the equilibrium of the relationship.
Sheldon Mitchell, Phoenix, AZ

Marriage is a contractual relationship, and the contract is dynamic and virtually always implicit. By implicit I mean that it is very rare that the parties express to each other that this is what I expect of you and our relationship. Spouses understand implicitly what they each want out of their marriage. By dynamic, I mean that it is always changing. As the marriage matures, each partner's values change and mature, and what they expect from the marriage changes. A divorce happens when there is a breach of this dynamic, implicit contract. To avoid divorce, each spouse needs to be sensitive to the changing dynamics and willing to adjust to those changes.
H. Joseph Gitlin, Woodstock, IL

The secret to a good marriage is to find your equal partner. Not someone who is going to dominate you or who you can dominate. The relationship has to be based on mutual respect, common purpose, and trust. When a couple has those things there ain't nobody who is going to break that marriage up.
Allen Zerman, St. Louis, MO

The starting point is to really see the marital relationship as the single most important relationship that a person has. A good marriage has full disclosure. Both parties need to identify what they want out of life and then continue that dialogue throughout their marriage. It doesn't take that much time, but it does take focus, and patience.
Ed Winer, Minneapolis, MN

Before you marry you need to have as much self awareness as possible. People who don't know who they are can't effectively share themselves with another person.
Elizabeth Scheffee, Portland, ME

No one is going to stay madly, passionately in love for 10, 20, or 30 years. Spouses need to have a sense of respect for each other and an appreciation for the things that they have accomplished together.
Martin Huddleston, Atlanta, GA

All of the people in your potential spouse's life, their family, their friends, and their friends to come, affect a marriage. Before you get married, take a careful look at your potential spouse's relationship with these other people.
Pamela Pierson, San Francisco, CA

After you are married, you need to continue to date your spouse.
Dennis Wasser, Los Angeles, CA

If you are married and having problems, go to the best marriage counselor that you can find. If you recognize a problem early on, you can generally fix it.
Sandra Morgan Little, Albuquerque, NM

If you follow these factors, your marriage has a good chance of working: commiting to open communication, getting pleasure out of making your spouse happy, subordinating your own needs to the other (this works both ways), and keeping romance and spontaneity in your relationship.
Sanford Ain, Washington, D.C.

Patience, patience, patience and forgiveness. Forgiveness not in the sense of superiority or being godlike, but from recognition that none of us is perfect and I am not going to judge you.

If you are married I can guarantee that you are going to have a rough patch; and you need to be perseverant enough, patient enough, to get

through it. If you go around clutching the resentment of the other's past sins to your breast, you probably aren't going to make it.
Tony Dick, Sacramento, CA

You need to continue to work to make your relationship good every day and never take your spouse or your relationship for granted. Find some rules for your relationship that keep it vital, alive, happy and desirous all the time. Do special things at random, like you would do if you were not married. Always try to give more than you get, and listen to what the other is saying responding in a non-hostile way. If you do this, you should remain on the long road to happiness and a wonderful, lasting relationship.
Stephen Kolodny, Beverly Hills, CA

Good communication is the most important ingredient to all successful relationships, and poor communication is the most significant torpedo to a good relationship. Communication is a two-way interaction. It requires an interested, respectful listener, and a respectful, specific speaker. Important issues (children, finances, work/assignments/tasks/expectations) should be discussed thoroughly before marriage and a consensus reached as to how these issues will be handled. A pattern of willingness to compromise, and to defer when needed, needs to be established by both persons before marriage.
Sandra Morris, San Diego, CA

Find someone who you have things in common with like sports, music, shows, theater, etc. As life goes on you must be willing to grow with the other person as they must be willing to grow with you. You must like each other's families as otherwise they can cause the most trauma in a marriage. Finally I believe you must learn and enjoy living with each other before you have children. It's better not to have children right away because you then bring a third person into the marriage before you are secure in yourselves.
Jack Rounick, Norristown, PA

Love, as with life, changes over the years. Our interests, likes and dislikes, and concept of life and love at 20 are infinitely different than they are at 50. When you experience problems, consult with a marriage counselor, or some other mental health professional that can help you and your spouse address the issues and problems in your relationship with an eye towards correcting them, rather than running away from them. No one ever said that marriage was easy.

Marshall Waller, Woodland Hills, CA

Unhappiness in a marriage is most often the result of control by one individual over another causing loss of identity and self-respect. To those about to be married (or married), my advice is to encourage the separate interests of your spouse. Support and nurture your loved one's individuality and creativity.

Joslin Davis, Winston-Salem, NC

Communication is the most essential factor to a strong relationship and it must begin before the wedding. For instance, the parties must discuss how they are going to handle their financial affairs even before the wedding invitations are sent. The lack of this understanding before the marriage leads to a certain level mistrust. Accusations that one party is hiding money from the other or that one party of spending more money than the other are generally the most commonplace.

Jon S. Summers, Los Angeles, CA

Aside from the obvious – making sure there is a good mutual respect in place – have a good pre-nuptial agreement. Many wars have been caused by miscalculation of entitlements and ambitions. A pre-nuptial agreement prevents this.

Raoul Lionel Felder, New York, NY

The following attorneys generously participated in the making of this book:

1) Sanford K. Ain, Washington, D.C.

2) Eleanor Breitel Alter, New York, NY

3) Wolfgang R. Anderson, Seattle, WA

4) Stephen R. Arnold, Birmingham, AL

5) Emily S. Bair, Atlanta, GA

6) Rita M. Bank, Washington, D.C.

7) Edward E. Bates, Jr., Atlanta, GA

8) Phyllis G. Bossin, Cincinnati, OH

9) Robert D. Boyd, Atlanta, GA

10) Eleanor Breitel Alter, New York, NY

11) Steven E. Briggs, Newport Beach, CA

12) Irwin Buter, Los Angeles, CA

13) Helen E. Christian, Salt Lake City, UT

14) Bruce A. Clemens, Beverly Hills, CA

15) Sharon L. Corbitt, Tulsa, OK

16) Bert L. Dart, Salt Lake City, Utah

17) Baxter L. Davis, Atlanta, GA

18) Joslin Davis, Winston-Salem, NC

19) Mabry C. De Buys, Seattle, WA

20) Anthony S. Dick, Sacramento, CA

21) David S. Dolowitz, Salt Lake City, UT

22) Shiel G. Edlin, Atlanta, GA

23) Marsha Elser, Miami, FL

24) Ike Vanden Eykel, Dallas, Texas

25) Raoul Lionel Felder, New York, NY

26) James H. Feldman, Chicago, IL

27) Patricia Ferrari, New York, NY

28) H. Michael Fields, Seattle, WA

29) Melvyn B. Frumkes, Miami, FL

30) Donn C. Fullenweider, Houston, TX

31) Saul M. Gelbart, Costa Mesa, CA

32) Janet A. George, Seattle, WA

33) H. Joseph Gitlin, Woodstock, IL

34) Herbert A. Glieberman, Chicago, IL

35) Lynne Z. Gold-Bikin, Norristown, PA

36) Corie M. Goldblum, Miami, FL

37) Darla J. Goodwin, Seattle, WA

38) Cynthia L. Greene, Miami, FL

39) Hanley M. Gurwin, Bloomfield Hills, MI

40) Stephen J. Harhai, Denver, CO

41) H. Martin Huddleston, Atlanta, GA

42) William L. Hunnicut, Denver, CO

43) Herndon Inge, Mobile, AL

44) Daniel J. Jaffe, Beverly Hills, CA

45) Lewis Kapner, West Palm Beach, FL

46) Mary J. Kelly, Denver, CO

47) Ellen Widen Kessler, New Orleans, LA

48) Stephen A. Kolodny, Beverly Hills, CA

49) Kenneth Koopersmith, Garden City, NY

50) Maurice Jay Kutner, Miami, FL

51) Steven R. Lake, Chicago, IL

52) Steven J. Lane, New Orleans, LA

53) David H. Lee, Boston, MA

54) Andrew Martin Leinoff, Coral Gables, FL

55) Ken H. Lester, Columbia, SC

56) Elizabeth Green Lindsey, Atlanta, GA

57) Sandra Morgan Little, Albuquerque, NM

58) Mary Johanna McCurly, Dallas, TX

59) Michael McCurley, Dallas, TX

60) Denise K. Mills, Denver, CO

61) Sheldon M. Mitchell, Phoenix, AZ

62) Sandra J. Morris, San Diego, CA

63) Robert J. Nachshin, Santa Monica, CA

64) Gerald L. Nissenbaum, Boston, MA

65) Herbert Palkovitz, Cleveland, OH

66) Pamela E. Pierson, San Francisco

67) Stacy D. Phillips, Los Angeles

68) JoAnn B. Reynolds, Portland, OR

69) Bernard B. Rinella, Chicago

70) Ronald A. Rosenfeld, Beverly Hills

71) Jack A. Rounick, Norristown, PA

72) David L. Sandor, Irvine, CA

73) Elizabeth J. Scheffee, Portland, Maine

74) Donald C. Schiller, Chicago, IL

75) John R. Schilling Newport Beach, CA

76) Philip G. Seastrom, Newport Beach

77) Norman M. Sheresky, New York, NY

78) Peter Sherman, Washington, D.C

79) Eric S. Spevak, Haddonfield, NJ

80) Carla F. Stern, Atlanta, GA

81) George S. Stern, Atlanta, GA

82) Lawrence Stotter, San Francisco, CA

83) Lowell H. Sucherman, San Francisco, CA

84) Jon S. Summers, Los Angeles, CA

85) Suzie Thorn, San Francisco, CA

86) Karen Tosh, Boston, MA

87) Sorrell Trope, Los Angeles, CA

88) Marna S. Tucker, Washington, D.C.

89) Marshall W. Waller, Woodland Hills, CA

90) David L. Walther, Santa Fe, NM

91) Dennis M. Wasser, Los Angeles, CA

92) Mary H. Wechsler, Seattle, WA

93) Scott N. Weston, Santa Monica, CA

94) Jacqueline A. Whisnant, Newport
Beach, CA

95) Joanne Ross Wilder, Pittsburgh, PA

96) Marshal S. Willick, Las Vegas, NV

97) Edward L. Winer, Minneapolis, MN

98) Marshall J. Wolf, Cleveland, OH

99) Errol Zavett, Chicago, IL

100) Allan H. Zerman, Clayton, MO

About the Author

Wendy Jaffe, daughter of prominent divorce attorney Daniel J. Jaffe, and niece of the late Judge Harry Jaffe, graduated from the University of California, Los Angeles in 1983, and from the McGeorge School of Law in 1986. Her legal career began as the supervising research attorney for the late Honorable John Cole. Following her clerkship, she spent several years practicing law, and also created and marketed a successful and highly publicized novelty item geared toward enhancing passion between couples. She resides in Los Angeles with her husband and two children.